Creative Ways to Teach Literacy

Creative Ways to Teach Literacy

Ideas for Children aged 3 to 11

Virginia Bower

Los Angeles | London | New Delhi
Singapore | Washington DC

SAGE Publications Ltd
1 Oliver's Yard
55 City Road
London EC1Y 1SP

SAGE Publications Inc.
2455 Teller Road
Thousand Oaks, California 91320

SAGE Publications India Pvt Ltd
B 1/I 1 Mohan Cooperative Industrial Area
Mathura Road
New Delhi 110 044

SAGE Publications Asia-Pacific Pte Ltd
33 Pekin Street #02-01
Far East Square
Singapore 048763

Library of Congress Control Number: 2010939350

British Library Cataloguing in Publication data

A catalogue record for this book is available from the British Library

ISBN 978-0-85702-045-1
ISBN 978-0-85702-046-8 (pbk)

Typeset by C&M Digitals (P) Ltd, Chennai, India
Printed in Great Britain by CPI Antony Rowe, Chippenham, Wiltshire
Printed on paper from sustainable resources

To Peter – who always manages to find the right words
To Mum and Dad for their support of
everything I do

Contents

Acknowledgements   ix
About the editor and contributors   xi
Introduction   xiii
Virginia Bower

Section 1   Narrative   1

1   *Enhancing children's writing*   3
    Virginia Bower

2   *An exploration of traditional tales*   12
    Caroline Tancock

3   *Writing from experience*   23
    Justine Earl

Section 2   Poetry   33

4   *Playground games as a foundation for literacy lessons*   35
    Sue Hammond and Karen Vincent

5   *Using poetic form: an approach to poetry writing in the primary classroom* 45
    Susan Barrett and Virginia Bower

6   *Poetry is slamming: different ways to perform poetry in primary schools*   55
    Andrew Lambirth

Section 3   Non-fiction   65

7   *Inspiring and enthusing children as readers and writers of non-fiction*   67
    Michael Green

8   *Lights, camera, action ... take 9!*   77
    Tracy Parvin

9   *Enhancing children's language acquisition and development through non-fiction* 86
    Virginia Bower

Index   97

Acknowledgements

Virginia
Thank you to all the people I worked with – staff, parents and children – at Cheriton Primary School.

Justine
Thanks to Marden school in Kent for allowing children to share their out of school texts.

Karen
Thank you to all of my colleagues and friends at Barming school in Kent for their help and encouragement.

Tracy
Thank you to the children of Class 5 Hernhill Primary School in Kent for their ability to engage in this project with enthusiasm, dedication and commitment; thank you also for not only making me smile, but laugh.

The case studies included in this publication are a composite of numerous children in various settings, complied over the authors' many years of experience, and are not specific to any one child, practitioner or setting.

About the editor and contributors

The editor

Virginia Bower is a Senior Lecturer in Primary Education at Canterbury Christ Church University. She teaches on both the undergraduate programme and on the full-time PGCE English course and is also part of the team who teach the Masters in Language and Literacy. Virginia is very keen to promote a love of literature in both children and university students and currently runs a reading group for undergraduate trainee teachers where children's literature is shared, studied and enjoyed. Her current research interests focus on first and second language acquisition and development.

The contributors

Susan Barrett is a Lecturer in the Department of Primary Education at Canterbury Christ Church University where she teaches undergraduate and postgraduate English and Professional Studies courses. This follows a classroom teaching career of 23 years, first as a secondary English teacher and later an upper Key Stage 2 teacher and deputy head. She is currently working towards her Masters in Literacy and Learning and has a keen interest in children's literature and its use in the classroom.

Justine Earl is a Senior Lecturer in Primary Education at Canterbury Christ Church University. She teaches on the various postgraduate routes into teaching, specialising in English and Primary Languages. She currently leads the full- and part-time PGCE English courses. She enjoys visiting students undertaking placements in the UK and abroad. Justine also teaches on the Masters in Language and Literacy programme, supervising teachers who are working to achieve their MA. Her other areas of interest include developing partnerships with schools.

Michael Green is a Senior Lecturer at Canterbury Christ Church University, where he leads the BA Primary Education module focusing on learning outside the classroom. In addition he teaches on a number of other modules, including Primary English and Professional Studies. Prior to joining ITE, Michael worked as assistant head teacher in a primary school in Medway. His current research interests include the potential use of outdoor learning opportunities for children and digital literacy practices.

Sue Hammond is a Senior Lecturer in the Department of Primary Education at Canterbury Christ Church University. She specialises in teaching English and Early Years and has acted as an educational consultant in Malaysia and India. Prior to joining the university, Sue taught in a range of primary schools over a period of more than twenty years. This included 14 years of teaching in a Reception class and her interest in researching and working with young children continues to be a passion.

Andrew Lambirth is Professor of Education in the School of Education at the University of Greenwich. He was previously Reader in Education at Canterbury Christ Church University. Andrew has written widely on the subject of literacy in primary schools. Titles include *Understanding Phonics and the Teaching of Reading* (Open University), *Creativity and Writing: Developing Voice and Verve in the Classroom* (Routledge) and *Literacy on the Left: Reform and Revolution* (Continuum). Before joining higher education, he taught in Peckham and Bermondsey in south London.

Tracy Parvin is a Senior Lecturer in Primary Education at Canterbury Christ Church University. She teaches on both the undergraduate programme and on the full-time PGCE English course. Not wanting to be left out of anything to do with the promoting of picture books, Tracy co-runs the students' reading group with Virginia! Her current research interests are focusing on the development of early reading teaching practices.

Caroline Tancock is a Senior Lecturer in the Department of Primary Education at Canterbury Christ Church University, where she is a member of the BA (Hons) Primary Education management team. She teaches on the undergraduate programme on a number of modules including English and Professional Studies. Prior to joining the university, Caroline worked in a primary school in the Medway area. Her current research interests include cultural influences upon reading experiences and attitudes.

Karen Vincent worked as a teacher for 18 years before recently taking up a post as a Senior Lecturer in the Department of Primary Education at Canterbury Christ Church University. She teaches across all of the Primary Programmes specialising in Early Years education. Her research interests include young children's perceptions of learning and the transition between Year R and Year 1.

Introduction

This book is a collaborative endeavour which arises from the desire of the primary English team at Canterbury Christ Church University more widely to disseminate ideas and beliefs about the teaching of literacy in primary schools, and to offer a range of perspectives relating to both theory and practice. According to Jim Cummins (2001: 1) theory and practice are:

> two-way and ongoing: practice generates theory, which, in turn, acts as a catalyst for new directions in practice, which then inform theory, and so on.

An awareness of theories and practices grounded in research is a prerequisite for teachers to enable them to feel empowered and confident in the classroom. Too often it is the case that, in relation to strategies, frameworks and policies, and not least through centralised professional development, teachers feel themselves to be constantly questioned and even undermined. Where this is the case, the consequent effect upon the planning and teaching process is hardly beneficial to the children.

This book seeks to argue that, if teachers are aware of and put into practice their own key principles, underpinned by theory and research, then not only will the children they teach prosper and achieve, but they will also be inspired and motivated to become lifelong learners. This in turn leads to secure, motivated teachers whose philosophies and pedagogies have their basis in robust research.

According to Craft (2005), the irony is that while the government exhorts teachers to be creative and innovative, parallel to this are messages dictating *what* should be taught and *how* this should be done, with the effect of 'reducing creativity in the teaching profession'. Creative teaching requires teachers to 'make learning more interesting, exciting and effective' (DfEE, 1999: 89) and for this to happen, we have to believe in ourselves and have the confidence to collaborate with, rather than coerce, the pupils (Cummins, 2001) and be prepared to learn together, enquiring and exploring, questioning and seeking, staying open to new ideas and practices.

The emphasis within this book is upon inspiring and enthusing children and teachers, linking theory and practice to encourage professionals to be both creative and original in their planning and teaching. The authors are aware, however, that within most primary schools some elements of the National Literacy Strategy (DfEE, 1998) and the Primary National Strategy (DfES, 2006) are significantly embedded in practice. This relates particularly to genre, and while there are increasing attempts to link literacy lessons with other areas of the curriculum, the 'units of work' still tend to be focused upon either narrative, poetry or non-fiction. The Strategy materials which have been produced contain useful material to support the teaching of these units, but care must be taken that materials are not accepted without questioning the theories that underlie their implementation. To do this is to run the risk of becoming 'task managers' or 'curriculum deliverers' rather than 'concept builders' who are informed and understand what they are teaching and why (Twiselton, 2000). This book attempts to achieve a balance: on the one hand remaining relevant to both student and qualified teachers by reflecting current practices in school, while on the other promoting a flexible and creative approach. It also carries the suggestion that boundaries between genres and subjects can easily be crossed to enhance both literacy teaching and learning as well as teaching across the curriculum.

The book is divided into nine chapters: three relating to narrative, three to poetry and three to non-fiction.

Chapter 1 looks at how using literature by a single author can allow children to find their own voice in their narrative writing. It emphasises the value of using high-quality texts and the importance of contextualising all teaching of specific literary conventions. The use of excellent texts – whether they be print-based, screen-based, films or other media – is one of the key themes permeating the book.

In **Chapter 2** the author explores a range of traditional tales from different cultures with a focus particularly on different versions of the Cinderella story. The chapter emphasises how traditional tales are universal and help children to deal with and make sense of human experience within their own cultures and those of others and appreciate the importance of cultural diversity. The strong story and language structure of such tales provides rich learning opportunities and the chapter will investigate how these texts can be used to engage children in narrative elements such as themes, characterisation, the setting and points of view.

Chapter 3 offers a very different perspective, as the author suggests that an explicit and continuous focus on genre may well restrict and constrain our young writers. While recognising that genre-led literacy can give children confidence to write in certain ways, this chapter reminds us that it is vital to recognise the fluid nature of the boundaries between genres and to be prepared to cross these boundaries to promote an exciting and innovative approach to literacy. Within the chapter a number of strategies and ideas are promoted, which encourage children to write for their own pleasure and purposes, both inside and outside of school.

Chapter 4 is the first of the three chapters focusing on poetry. The authors explore children's experiences with playground games, narrative, songs, chants and rhymes and discuss how these might be used in the classroom to enhance the children's understanding of rhythm, rhyme and other poetic devices. A case study is presented and ideas are drawn from this, suggesting how, by respecting children's existing knowledge and understanding and by acknowledging and embracing their lives outside school, we can have a positive impact on their social and emotional development and early reading and writing skills.

Chapter 5 looks at ways of supporting children's poetry writing in the classroom through the use of existing poetic forms. It begins with a consideration of differing views on this subject from leading writers, moving on to offer practical advice for classroom approaches. Samples of children's writing are offered in an attempt to demonstrate how using poetic forms can still liberate the 'voice' of the young poet. The needs of different groups of children including the EAL learner are also considered. The chapter concludes with a call to allow children to experience a wide range of poetic forms in order to be empowered in their own writing.

Chapter 6 focuses upon performing poetry in primary classrooms. The author argues that performing poetry should be an integral part of a school day because it is enjoyable and rich in opportunities to learn about poetry and the world. He emphasises the fact that performance poetry – with its combination of movement, language and talk – is a mode of learning that has a firm theoretical foundation. The author contends that the performance of poetry does not always require an audience and goes on to create a broad typology for performing poetry.

Chapter 7, the first of three chapters devoted to non-fiction, explores how creative teachers support children in becoming successful and enthusiastic readers and writers of non-fiction. It highlights the importance of choosing the right text and the need to embed children's experiences of reading and writing non-fiction in meaningful contexts which relate to their interests and experiences both in and outside of school. Suggestions are made relating to how a cross-curricular approach can be adopted for the teaching of non-fiction and the role of ICT is discussed. Throughout the chapter there is a focus on the teacher's role in the teaching of non-fiction at a practical level and the process of teaching children about non-fiction within literacy.

Chapter 8 is based on an extended cross-curricular project which focused on non-fiction texts, culminating in the production of a digital video. The author suggests that through the use of film-making, children's experience of non-fiction can be enhanced as they cross subject boundaries and begin to develop both their social and cognitive skills. The chapter gives examples from a project to highlight both the benefits and the potential difficulties of this approach to non-fiction. Three key themes emerge: group work, interaction and inclusion; immersion in texts; knowledge of the audience and purpose – and these are discussed in some depth.

Chapter 9 looks at the specific challenges for all pupils, but particularly those for whom English is an additional language, which non-fiction texts present. The author highlights and discusses principles and practical strategies which teachers can adopt to support EAL pupils, to enable them to enjoy non-fiction and to allow them to access, capture and record information from and respond effectively to this genre. Also included is a consideration of the implications for teachers for children learning EAL and how the strategies discussed can be of benefit to all learners.

References

Craft, A. (2005) *Creativity in Schools: Tensions and Dilemmas.* Oxford: RoutledgeFalmer.

Cummins, J. (2001) *Language, Power and Pedagogy.* Clevedon: Multilingual Matters.

DfEE (1998) *The National Literacy Strategy: Framework for Teaching.* Sudbury: DfEE.

DfEE (1999) *All Our Futures: Creativity, Culture and Education.* Report of the National Advisory Committee on Creative and Cultural Education: Sudbury: DfEE.

DfES (2006) *Primary Framework for Literacy and Mathematics.* Nottingham: DfES.

Twiselton, S. (2000) 'Seeing the wood for the trees: the National Literacy Strategy and Initial Teacher Education – pedagogical content knowledge and the nature of subjects', *Cambridge Journal of Education*, 30 (3): 391–403.

Section 1

Narrative

1

Enhancing children's writing

Virginia Bower

Chapter Overview

In this chapter I suggest that the study of the works of a single author not only fulfils a range of objectives but can also provide a deeper insight into how children's engagement with texts might 'empower' them and thereby influence their independent writing. It is therefore a 'way in' to literature for all age groups and abilities, and places the emphasis on the importance of the texts themselves, how these texts can be utilised as scaffolds and how texts can be used to contextualise the technical aspects of writing. The chapter emphasises the importance of a flexible and creative approach when planning to use the works of a single author, demonstrating how, given the time and opportunity, children can use the words they hear and read to find their own distinctive voice. The ideas and examples I use are taken from lessons taught during units of work which focused upon stories by Kevin Crossley-Holland. These lessons, and the resulting conversations with children and the work they produced, revealed the unique ways in which individuals reacted to the study of texts by a single author. For some it gave them a 'voice' which provided a scaffold for their own written work. For others, however, it merely provided them with the freedom within which they were able to play with and subvert existing textual structures, manipulating them for their own use. It is hoped that as this chapter is read, three key themes will emerge, which are all inextricably linked. The first of these is the power of text and how children can be empowered through reading to find their own 'voice'. The second theme relates to the impact of powerful literature on children's writing, and finally the third is the idea that 'texts can teach' – a recognition of the implicit nature of contextualisation in the teaching of all aspects of writing.

The power of text

One of our roles and responsibilities as educators is to appreciate the power of texts and recognise how, when children are given the opportunities to engage more deeply with texts, they can use this power to find a voice, both oral and written. As practitioners working within a classroom setting, I feel it is vital that we find keys to help unlock children's writing potential, not simply to raise attainment with regard to national assessment, but to provide children with the essential tools for life:

> The spoken and written word are vital to life in the world outside school, and provide the medium for nearly all teaching and learning in the primary school and beyond.
> (Cremin and Dombey, 2007: 14)

It is often said that reading and writing are inextricably linked, developing in children as 'a holistic package' (Flynn, 2007: 143). A general assumption might be that 'what children write reflects the nature and quality of their reading' (Barrs and Cork, 2001: 35). It could therefore be concluded that the better the reader, the better the writer. Martin (2003) recognises that children are labelled as strong or weak readers and suggests that the focus should be placed more on whether a reader is *experienced* or *inexperienced* in relation to reading and that it is this which will impact on writing. He questions whether the difficulties connected with raising writing standards are based on children not reading *enough*:

> They are not experienced enough as readers to write like a reader. (Martin, 2003: 15)

It is therefore essential that pupils have the opportunity to hear, and read for themselves, a wide range of texts from the chosen author, so that they are able to become 'experienced' readers (even if only within this narrow field). One of my concerns with using a single author was that some children might not enjoy the work of Kevin Crossley-Holland and would therefore be subjected to literature which did not interest them. (Fortunately, this never emerged as an issue, as the children thoroughly enjoyed the literature.) Although there is no guarantee that the work of a particular author will engage and stimulate an entire class of pupils, there are a number of strategies you can employ to promote an appreciation of the chosen author:

- Select an author who has the potential to inspire and engage young readers and find websites/magazine articles/autobiographies and biographies relating to the author so that children can get to 'know' them.

- Choose an author who has written a wide selection of books, including short stories (which could be translated for children with English as an additional language), picture books and, illustrated stories, where the words are reinforced with powerful images enabling all children to access the meaning more easily, and more complex and demanding stories to engage the more able.

- Choose texts which are strong models for children's own writing, where the author's voice permeates the pages and where language is used effectively.

During a single author study, children need to be immersed in a wide range of high-quality literature, within which familiar themes, rhythms, structures and linguistic patterns can be identified and explored. I chose Kevin Crossley-Holland, not only because of the range of literature he has written, but because I consider his stories to be 'strong' and 'powerful'. To define this type of text might be to see them as those which 'challenge and make demands on readers; they require readers to become active and involved in the world of the text' (Barrs and Cork, 2001: 36). This activity and involvement can be further encouraged by reading aloud – 'bringing the text alive and lifting it off the page' (Barrs and Cork, 2001: 72) – and this is a vital ingredient of successful and creative literacy teaching and learning. When I talked to children in my class about this, they specifically referred to *my* voice – the voice of the reader of the stories, '*We love it when you do the voices!*' They felt that having the stories read *to* them helped them with their writing; one child explained this as follows:

> Well, you say good words and you speak the persons out and you describe the setting.

According to Barrs and Cork, reading aloud to children allows them to 'take on the whole feeling and rhythm of a text' (Barrs and Cork, 2001: 116) and it is possible that when this child says 'and you speak the persons out' he means that the characters are made real by the very act of reading their words aloud. Being able to hear these voices is seen by some as having a significant impact on children's writing:

'Our written voices are intimately linked to the oral voices of others' (Grainger et al., 2005: 25). The 'voice' might be the voice of the author, that of his characters, the voice of the person reading aloud, or perhaps the child's own voice inside their head which reflects the material of the text. The oral text can facilitate a 'way in', providing 'the stimulus and motivation to explore printed texts' (Reedy and Lister, 2007: 5) and makes the young *writer* considerate of potential *readers* of their own work. In this way, they can be made aware of the communicational implications of their own writing; that they are writing for an audience for whom the text needs to make sense and who need to be stimulated.

It is vital that you, in your role as teacher, are aware of the considerable impact that reading aloud can have upon children and therefore it is a skill that needs developing. Here are some important issues to consider when reading aloud:

- Wherever possible, choose texts which you enjoy – your reading will be much more animated!

- Use a range of voices for different characters so that children are aware of who is speaking at any time. This does not mean that you have to be able to speak in different accents (I am hopeless with this!) – you can make your voice higher or lower, louder or softer, bossy or mild, etc. I was always amazed when children asked me to 'do the voices' because I did not feel that I was particularly skilled in this area, but the small changes I made to my voice clearly made a big difference to the children's understanding and enjoyment.

- Practise in advance so that you feel confident with the material and can choose places where you might pause or ask the children to predict or perhaps introduce some process drama to explore a particular aspect of the story.

The impact of powerful literature on children's writing

According to Benton and Fox:

> Writing and reading are indivisible. The writer's sense of audience and the reader's sense of textual voice complement each other and form a social bond. (Benton and Fox, 1985: 20)

If this is the case, then literature could be seen as the key to quality writing. Children need access to what Margaret Meek would describe as 'texts that teach' (Meek, 1988). These kinds of texts provide a model of quality language and composition, while allowing the reader opportunities to interpret the text in their own very personal way. In my discussions with children following reading aloud sessions, they would often quote directly from the text they had been listening to. In one particular instance, a child recited the phrase 'slice of moon' from a Crossley-Holland story, because this use of language had appealed to her. However, when the child then went on to complete a piece of writing linked with the story she had heard, rather than just reproducing the phrase, she manipulated and reinterpreted it to satisfy her own requirements (see below).

> She looked back to see if Storm was still there but no he had disappeared but yet the slim slice of moon had not changed position! It seemed she hadn't moved till Storm arrived! But where did Storm go?

The insertion of the word 'slim' has two effects: it subtly alters the meaning of the sentence and it uses alliteration to lend the sentence cadence. This indicates an ability to recognise the prosodic element within written composition and points towards a growing awareness of the power of language and the personal power imbued upon an author as they take control over somebody else's words. The ideas and writing have clearly been influenced by the language of Crossley-Holland, providing the child with the necessary literary equipment to enable her to transform her knowledge and produce her own original creation.

A single-author study should ensure that children have constant exposure to high-quality texts. It is also vital to leave time to discuss what they have heard or read for themselves and to make any relevant links to their own life experiences. As a result of these strategies you should start to notice some significant influences upon their writing. These might include any or all of the following:

- *Hearing your own voice (as the reader) in their written words.* This can be quite disconcerting! If, for example, you have allotted a 'gruff' or 'squeaky' voice to a particular character, young writers will often use this in their direct speech, i.e. 'Help!' she cried in a high-pitched squeaky voice.

- *Hearing the voices of the characters within the narrative.* If the texts used are of a high quality with well-drawn characters with whom children can relate, then you will 'feel' their presence within children's writing.

- *Hearing their own very personal and unique voice, reflecting their experience of life.* If children have the opportunity to identify and discuss any links between the literature presented and their own lives, this will emerge through their writing. I shall explore this further below.

To create effective and meaningful pieces of writing, children need to draw upon their own experiences and link these with what they have read. The example below shows a good example of this. This piece of writing was based on the short story 'Wrestling' by Crossley-Holland.

> Princess Sophie was having a stroll around the castle when she realised she was very lonely. Her fiancée Dan, a football player, had gone to Manchester for a huge football tournament; this meant a lot to Dan because he could become very famous but nothing in the world even a football tournament would let Dan stop getting married to his beautiful fiancée! Sophie! He promised Sophie he would be back in time for a fantastic wedding!

Crossley-Holland's story opening is very brief, merely setting the scene with little detail. This child's version, in contrast, fills in the gaps left by the original author, in a way which evidently pleases her as she examines the emotions experienced by the main character and the reasons behind their loneliness. This detail serves several purposes. It allows the writer to add an extra character to her narrative, who, although he never appears, provides the reason for the Princess's loneliness and adds an element of romance to the tale. Not only this, by making this character a famous footballer, the writer is also modernising and updating the original version, attempting to appeal to a wider audience with subject matter which is relevant and popular, linking fantasy and real life:

> Transformations from life are a part of most stories they tell. (Fox, 1993: 16)

Using football as the key theme shows that the child has thought ahead to the main part of her narrative, where, instead of wrestling, the animals have to score goals to decide who is to live with the Princess in the castle. The original story has provided the means by which the child has been able to plan ahead; she was aware of the main theme of the original tale and that her story should echo this theme. However, she also knew that she needed to find her own voice within the new narrative; the original story has provided a platform from which she has been able to develop this voice.

By creating their own versions of stories, developing writers are able to produce what Ellis and Mills (2002) describes as a 'scripted' story, using an existing narrative, changing various elements and making it their own. Lamott (1994) describes the adoption of the style of an author as a useful 'prop' which a writer borrows until it has to be returned:

> And it might just take you to the thing that is not on loan, the thing that is real and true, your own voice. (Lamott, 1994: 195)

To reinforce the powerful nature of texts, it is good practice to *re-read* stories where possible, to enable the children to 'soak up' the language and rhythms which are a significant aspect of a writer's style. Following a re-reading, I would find that children were able to remember whole sections of text and they appeared to retain them for a long time afterwards, providing them with prompts and support with their own writing. Fox (1993) believes that prosodic features – for example, repetition and rhyme – have more influence over narrative structure than the plot and certainly the repetitive nature of many of Crossley-Holland's stories influenced the children's own writing. I would like to illustrate this with one particular example.

One of the pupils in my class, despite enjoying stories and being read to, always struggled when faced with a writing task and would often sit for long lengths of time producing little or nothing on paper, if not supported. When she did put pen to paper, it was often followed by copious amounts of erasing and starting all over again. During this unit of work, however, the child produced three pieces of writing which far exceeded her normal attempts. All three compositions contain references to the original texts, whether they be direct 'liftings' or connected closely either by style, language or content. When she was asked to write in the style of Crossley-Holland the child was clearly able to find a narrative voice which echoed the literature of the author, indicating that she was strongly influenced by the literature she had experienced. However, there is more to this influence than merely her ability to adopt the features of Crossley-Holland's work. It would appear that this influence acted as a catalyst for her own ideas. The following extract below is taken from her final piece of writing in the unit of work, where the task was to write a sequel to a story called 'Storm':

> 'I'm going in the car are you coming with me or not' shouted Dr Grant when Annie was half way down the road. Annie jumped eagerly into the car and relaxed for the first time that night. In a twinkling they'd crossed the ford and got to the house. Just before Willa had her baby! 'What a night!' said Annie.

This extract is the last paragraph of the child's sequel. The first paragraph contains many references to the original text, including some direct quotes. The extract above, however, is very different. The child's own voice is beginning to emerge with the clever use of words such as 'jumped eagerly' to reveal a character's state of mind. The phrase 'in a twinkling', although not original from a world-view, does not originate from Crossley-Holland's story and is effectively used by the writer to signify the short lapse of time which has passed. The final phrase – '"What a night!" said Annie' – reveals an appreciation of how the character would have been feeling and in just three words expresses a depth of understanding which is quite extraordinary. In this extract, the child has transcended her earlier dependency upon the literature she has been read and has found the confidence to find her own voice. She has overcome the writing 'block' which had prevented her in the past from producing writing which met her own exacting standards.

The importance of contextualisation

Rosen (1989) believes that children's perceptions of 'good' writing (gained undoubtedly from teacher and other adult expectations) can prevent them from writing because they are concerned that they cannot fulfil this expectation. I would concur with this, and I believe that this perception is exacerbated when the more technical aspects of writing are taught in a decontextualised way. As a result of this 'discrete' teaching, children might see 'good' writing as that which contains particular literary turns of phrase or conventions such as the effective use of adjectives, adverbs, similes or metaphors, without realising that the manner in which these devices are used is crucial to producing effective writing. Because of the nature of a single-author study, it should be possible to teach the technical aspects of writing through the many and varied texts which have been selected. During my own teaching, I was determined to do just that and yet, as you will see from the discussion below, the results were very mixed.

Here is a piece of writing produced during the single-author unit of work:

> 'Oh my, this storm surely can't get any worse' said Annie. She shivered. She was as cold as Antarctica and the rain was slashing her face. When Annie caught her breath she tearfully rang the doorbell. No answer. She tried again. Still no answer. She slammed her fist on the door and Dr Grant's wife opened the pale green door!

When I read this piece, I could hear the child's own narrative voice permeating through the language and style, and his use of short sentences to build tension reflects the way in which Kevin Crossley-Holland often creates his effects. These aspects pleased me! What was interesting, however, was his explicit use of specific literary conventions – the simile relating to Antarctica, the use of the adverb 'tearfully', the adjectives to describe the door – all of which seemed to indicate that the writer was very conscious of what could be seen as 'school expectations' and which, for me, leant the piece a rather contrived air.

When asked what effect the story reading had had upon his own writing, the child commented predominantly on the technical aspects of the literature studied, as opposed to the storyline, characters or other textual features. Perhaps he believed this was what I as teacher wanted to hear – after all it was I who would be marking his work!

Frater (2004) suggests that the gap between reading and writing has been exacerbated by the explicit teaching of grammar and the mechanical aspects of writing. He believes that the enriching experience of the reading of powerful texts may reduce the need for more formalised teaching. My project revolved around the use of powerful texts and the contextualisation of any teaching relating to the writing process. Despite this, at times the children's writing reflected a desire to include what could be perceived as specifically taught conventions in order to produce work which conformed to the notion of 'good' writing. This made me aware that, however powerful the text, the role of the teacher and how they choose to use texts is crucial and the importance of embedding the technical aspects of the writing process within a whole text framework cannot be overstated. In this way, it is hoped that young writers do not lose the all important focus on composition and producing writing which provides enjoyment and satisfaction.

Here are some ideas to promote children's writing which reflect the original thoughts of the writer and yet address the need to teach the technical elements of the writing process:

- Select high-quality texts which (a) use a wide range of language effectively; (b) demonstrate a range of punctuation which impacts upon how the text is read and (c) have strong structures which children can use as models for their own writing.

- Have a good knowledge and understanding of the texts you are going to use. This will allow you to draw attention to specific features and discuss how and why they are used at particular times.

- Put the focus on *why* the author has used a certain word or piece of punctuation and why they have chosen to start a new paragraph at a particular point in the narrative. Take time to discuss this and to explore the impact this has on the way the text is read.

Conclusion

Bakhtin (1986) writes that:

> With a creative attitude toward language, there are no voiceless words that belong to no one. (Bakhtin, 1986: 124)

By selecting and immersing children in the works of a single author, we should be able to promote this 'creative attitude toward language' and thereby allow children to find a voice which belongs to them from the many voices to be found in the literature studied. As teachers, it is vital to realise the implications of the current mode of assessment, but it is also crucial to look beyond the potential narrowness of this focus and to consider the significant role one plays in the lives of the children in our care:

> Literacy can and should be about involvement and enjoyment, and has the potential to create lifelong readers and writers, as well as developing their competence. (Nicholson, 2006: 19)

If writing is not to become merely a 'product' by which children are measured (Packwood and Messenheimer, 2003), it needs to be used as a 'reflective, cognitive tool' whereby children explore their inner selves and the world around them while 'sharing and critically evaluating knowledge, beliefs, attitudes, culture, traditions and so on' (Packwood and Messenheimer, 2003: 145). Practitioners have a responsibility to find and utilise 'powerful literature' in order to provide children with excellent models for their own writing. Included in this is the importance of providing enough examples of writing by a single author so that children have the opportunity to choose preferred texts rather than have texts presented to them arbitrarily. If total immersion is to occur, there needs to be *enough* literature for children to take part in shared, guided and independent reading, providing them with opportunities to absorb the 'sounds, patterns and nuances' of the texts (Barrs and Cork, 2001: 36). Although it is not possible to predict that every child in a class will enjoy stories by a particular author, if the chosen writer has produced a reasonable quantity of literature, with a variety of themes and subject matter, it is hoped that most children will find something that appeals to them. If it is possible to fully engage the children with the works of a single author, then this can have a significant impact upon their writing:

> Keenness for the work of a particular writer can be a great motivator for our own writing and studying the work of a writer in some depth – as avid series readers know – can be very satisfying. (Bearne, 2002: 90)

(Continued)

(Continued)

Texts and authors can be chosen from a range of sources including online material, films, picture books, short stories, novels, poems and non-fiction. Although this chapter appears within the section entitled 'Narrative', it is important to consider how genre boundaries within literacy can be crossed to provide children with a 'broad and rich curriculum' (Rose, 2006) based upon high-quality literature. Given a choice, children might select a favourite poet and explore a range of poems in order to help them to find their own poetic voice; they might investigate non-fiction texts in the form of biographies and autobiographies to provide them with additional background information; and they might compare paper-based and on-screen texts analysing the impact and effectiveness of both. The study of the works of a single author is relevant and useful for children of all ages and abilities. With the proliferation of wonderful picture books available and the easy access to online material, it should be possible to provide children, from a very early age, with texts which they can enjoy and which will enable them to find their own voice, both within the classroom and the wider world.

Something to read

The seminal text *The Reader in the Writer* by Myra Barrs and Valerie Cork (published by CLPE, 2001) provides excellent case studies showing how the reading of texts and the use of drama has an impact on children's writing.

Something to think about

It is important to provide opportunities for children to make links between their reading and their lives outside of school. In this chapter I have emphasised the need to give children opportunities to discuss any links and how this can impact upon their writing. Think of some other ways by which you can promote links between home and school and how you can encourage children to draw on their existing knowledge and understanding of the world and use this in their written work.

Something to try

Select an author (preferably someone whose work you are not familiar with). Find out as much as you can about the author, making a note of where you find any information. Locate at least ten pieces of literature they have written and immerse yourself in their style, making notes of any significant features within their writing. If you find that their texts appeal, try them out in the classroom! Good luck and enjoy!

References

Bakhtin, M. M. (1986) *Speech Genres and Other Late Essays*. Austin, TX: University of Texas Press.

Barrs, M. and Cork, V. (2001) *The Reader in the Writer*. London: Centre for Language in Primary Education.

Bearne, E. (2002) *Making Progress in Writing*. London: RoutledgeFalmer.

Benton, M. and Fox, G. (1985) *Teaching Literature Nine to Fourteen*. Oxford: Oxford University Press.

Cremin, T. and Dombey, H. (2007) *Handbook of Primary English in Initial Teacher Education*. Cambridge: NATE/UKLA.

Ellis, S. and Mills, C. (eds) (2002) *Connecting, Creating: New Ideas in Teaching Writing*. Royston: UK Reading Association.

Flynn, N. (2007) 'What do effective teachers of literacy do? Subject knowledge and pedagogical choices for literacy', *Literacy*, 41 (3): 137–47.

Fox, C. (1993) *At the Very Edge of the Forest: The Influence of Literature on Storytelling by Children*. London: Cassell.

Frater, G. (2004) 'Improving Dean's writing: or, what shall we tell the children?', *Literacy*, 38 (2): 78–83.

Grainger, T., Goouch, K. and Lambirth, A. (2005) *Creativity and Writing: Developing Voice and Verve in the Classroom*. London and New York: Routledge.

Lamott, A. (1994) *Bird by Bird: Some Instructions on Writing and Life*. New York and San Francisco: Pantheon Books.

Martin, T. (2003) 'Minimum and maximum entitlements: literature at Key Stage 2', *Reading* (now called *Literacy*), 37 (1): 14–17.

Meek, M. (1988) *How Texts Teach What Readers Learn*. Stroud: Thimble.

Nicholson, D. (2006) 'Putting literature at the heart of the literacy curriculum', *Literacy*, 40 (1): 11–22.

Packwood, A. and Messenheimer, T. (2003) 'Back to the future: developing children as writers', in E. Bearne, H. Dombey and T. Grainger (eds), *Classroom Interactions in Literacy*, Open University Press, pp. 144–56.

Reedy, D. and Lister, B. (2007) '"Busting with blood and gore and full of passion": the impact of an oral retelling of the Iliad in the primary classroom', *Literacy*, 41 (1): 3–10.

Rose, J. (2006) *Independent Review of the Teaching of Early Reading*. Nottingham: DfES.

Rosen, M. (1989) *Did I hear you write?*, 2nd edn. Nottingham: Five Leaves.

Children's Literature

Crossley-Holland, K. (1998) *SHORT! A Book of Very Short Stories*. Oxford: Oxford University Press.

2

An exploration of traditional tales

Caroline Tancock

Chapter Overview

In this chapter, I will explore a range of traditional tales from different cultures with a focus particularly on different versions of the Cinderella story. The chapter emphasises how traditional tales are universal and help children to deal with and make sense of human experience and develop an insight into human behaviour. The strong story and language structure of such tales provide rich learning opportunities and as such the chapter will investigate how these texts can be used to engage children in narrative elements such as themes, characterisation, the setting and points of view. A range of different activities will be considered with an emphasis on oracy, drama and role-play together with some suggestions for a cross-curricular approach. The chapter will also explore how teachers can use literature from around the world to provide children with the opportunity to develop an understanding and insight into their own culture and those of others and appreciate the importance of cultural diversity. The role of oral storytelling and its learning opportunities will be examined including how it provides children with English as an additional language with the confidence to discuss their own cultural experiences in the classroom and the opportunity to use their home language.

Types of tales

The term 'traditional tales' immediately brings to mind classic stories of our childhoods such as *Snow White*, *The Three Little Pigs* and *Cinderella*. In reality there are a vast number of traditional tales which extend worldwide and which can be drawn upon for use in the classroom. By definition, traditional tales are stories belonging to the oral tradition of storytelling. They are tales which have been passed from generation to generation across many different cultures with each story changed by the traditions and history of the culture in which they have developed. These tales have stood the test of time, provide immense pleasure to each successive generation and continue to provide the inspiration for popular films.

Traditional tales encompass a wide range of different narratives – myths, legends, folk tales, fairy stories and fables. It is worth briefly analysing the features of these, although it is important to recognise that some stories can include aspects of more than one narrative. Myths and legends, for example, can often be intertwined such as the stories in the Odyssey, where it can be difficult to distinguish between the mythic and legendary aspects. Fairy tales can have mythical elements and are also often described as folk tales. Despite the blurring of the boundaries, all traditional tales have a common theme in their desire to deal with and make sense of human experience.

Myths

These are the oldest stories and originate from the desire to explain how the world was created and natural phenomena such as the seasons and the cycle of day and night. They also have links to religious rites, spiritual beliefs and the ideals of the culture from which they originated and would have been told originally as if true. Myths often include stories and conflicts between gods and goddesses depicting the struggle between good and evil. In western cultures the most well known myths are probably those of the Ancient Greeks. But there are many others that can be utilised in the classroom. The Indian myths of the Mahabharata and the Ramayana tell the stories of the Hindu gods and goddesses and were often sung and danced as well as told orally. The Mesopotamian myth, *The Epic of Gilgamesh*, has a common theme with the Christian story of Noah – that of flooding. Norse myths and Irish myths such as the story of *Oisin and the land of Tír na nÓg* and creation myths from around the world such as the aboriginal tale *How the Sun Came into the World* have parallel stories in many other cultures.

Legends

Legends tell stories about heroes and brave deeds and are often based upon characters who are believed to have actually existed, for example King Arthur. There is some debate, however, as to the extent of the factual information; for example, there is some disagreement as to the existence of the legendary hero Robin Hood. There can, however, be no doubt that these tales, if based on any elements of truth, have been greatly exaggerated and the inclusion of fantastical beasts such as dragons, unicorns and chimeras in many legends has contributed to this.

Fables

Fables are short stories which have a clear moral message. The characters are usually animals, which are used to satirise human behaviour. The most well known of fables were written by Aesop and include tales such as *The Hare and the Tortoise*. Many cultures have their own versions of fables such as the African tale *The Leopard and the Hare*.

Folk tales

Folk tales are, as the name suggests, stories 'of the people', which have been passed from one generation to the next in the need to share wisdom and experience. There are differing views as to the origin of folk tales. Some believe that they developed spontaneously hundreds of thousands of years ago in different parts of the world. Others claim that they originated in India and were then passed around the world, which accounts for the similarities in the tales across cultures. In France in the seventeenth century, ladies of the court told each other stories in literary salons. These were then published by Charles Perrault in 1697 in *Histoires ou contes du temps passé*, and included versions of *Cinderella*, *Sleeping Beauty* and *Little Red Riding Hood*. However, the stories at this time were not told with children in mind and were created for an adult audience.

Many of the best-loved folk tales today are based on those told by Jacob and Wilhelm Grimm. Again they were not originally intended for young people, but proved to be popular with children and as such stories such as *Rumpelstiltskin* and *Hansel and Gretel* were edited to make them more child friendly. Folk tales from around the world can include a 'trickster' character, often an animal, who achieves success following a trick or quick-wittedness, for example Anancy (originally from Africa) and Baba Yaga (from Russia). Easy access to a wide range of folk tales makes them ideal for teaching and learning and are therefore going to be the focus of this chapter.

Fairy stories

Fairy stories as a term is often used generically to include folk tales. These stories do not always include a fairy as a character but usually contain magical, enchanting or supernatural elements. The main difference between a fairy story and a folk tale is that a fairy story is the imaginative work of one writer. Examples include stories such as *The Snow Queen* by Hans Christian Anderson and *The Happy Prince* by Oscar Wilde.

Although traditional tales are told around the world and have their own diversity, they also share common patterns, themes and plots. Some of this can be attributed to humans travelling the world, picking up stories and then changing them to fit in with their own culture. But it can also be 'explained by humankind's universal need to understand their surroundings and by common human characteristics' (Goodwin, 2008: 44).

Themes, structure and language

Traditional tales can enable children to develop an insight into human behaviour as they access stories about complex and archetypal issues common to 'real' life. Themes in traditional tales include: good and evil, rich and poor, young and old, beauty and ugliness, the origins of the earth and man, the supernatural, the quest to test individual skill and self-discovery (Grainger, 1997). They also allow children to explore moral and ethical issues such as justice and injustice and the reasons for a character's choices and behaviours. Bettleheim (1991) argues that traditional tales encourage children to deal with the dilemmas of growing up and play a significant role in their emotional development. Traditional tales also enable understanding between cultures to develop, as the themes involved are universal:

> For, in spite of apparent differences – cultural, racial, religious – it is the same emotions which move people worldwide: joy, pain, sorrow, fear, hope, hate, love. The themes are universal. We share a common humanity. (Beulah Candappa (1989), in Grainger, 1997: 27)

The oral nature of traditional tales means that they are memorable and as a result they have a strong story and language structure. Traditional tales have distinctive story patterns, constant characters and strong narrative structures. The language is rich with symbolism, imagery, metaphors, intertextuality and divergent meanings. They contain a strong rhythm, repetition and sometimes rhyme and this is why it is important that children are given the opportunity to hear the stories, play with them through retelling and join in with the patterns of the language.

Traditional tales are, however, not without their critics, in particular concerning their stereotypical representation of gender roles. The women in the tales are often depicted as victims or helpless and vulnerable waiting for a strong man to rescue them, while the men are portrayed as strong, capable and dominant. But this can be a focus of discussions in the classroom and children can be helped to challenge these stereotypes and deconstruct the text in order to explore the meanings behind such gender roles.

Exploring Cinderella stories from different cultures

There are hundreds of versions of the Cinderella story worldwide and the different versions provide rich texts to explore with children. The majority of children will be familiar with the story of Cinderella, even if it is just from the Walt Disney film version. Early discussions might include identifying key elements of the story: stepmother, two stepsisters, a ball, the lost slipper, etc. ... The children could take part in a group retelling of the tale with each child adding a small portion of the story. This would also be a timely opportunity to talk about the experiences of telling a story aloud and about the oral tradition of traditional tales and their evolution over time and cultures. The original tale by Charles Perrault could be shared or the Grimm brothers' version, also known as *Aschenputtel*.

Versions of Cinderella from other cultures are wide ranging. In this chapter I make reference to: *The Rough-Face Girl* by Rafe Martin, *Mufaro's Beautiful Daughters* by John Steptoe, *The Persian Cinderella* by Shirley Climo, *The Twelve Months* – a Slavic traditional tale – and *The Three Rival Brothers* – an African tale. *The Three Rival Brothers* has some of the elements of the Cinderella story but with a reversal of gender. There is a strong theme of sibling rivalry in this tale as the three brothers fight for the hand in marriage of the chief's daughter and the tale ends with a question – 'Who should marry her and get to rule the kingdom?' The opportunities for discussions on the reversal of gender and gender in general are wide ranging and this text will be discussed again later in the section on drama.

Setting the scene for telling the stories will develop a good storytelling atmosphere. How the scene is introduced will depend upon the story being told. For example, if the *Rough-Face Girl* is the chosen text then the children can sit in a circle to the gentle beating of a drum representing the heart beat of the Native American people. A campfire could be made using wood and paper flames for the children to sit around for the telling of *Mufaro's Beautiful Daughters* or the teller could be sat outside a made-up tent for the tale of *The Persian Cinderella*. An oral telling of the story would make the whole experience more authentic but the written text could also be shared.

Following the sharing of the traditional tales the children could be set the task of considering the plot, characters and setting. For *the Rough-Face Girl* they might consider the strength of the 'good character' in the story. A list could be made of the good and bad qualities of each of the characters. Actions of the characters could be compared together with how they affected others. For example, children could identify positive and negative traits of the characters of Nyasha and Manyara in *Mufaro's Beautiful Daughters*.

The setting of the stories will provide a good opportunity to discuss the culture from which the story originates. For example, in *the Rough-Face Girl* discussions could focus upon the qualities in the story which make it unique to the Native

American culture, such as the symbolism of the animals and the Great Spirit. The setting of 'the women's quarters' in *The Persian Cinderella* could generate much discussion about the Islamic culture and differences with western cultures.

Elements of folk tales could be identified in the various versions: magic, good versus evil and the lessons of the stories. Discussion of morals and lessons found in stories from different cultures are valuable because they are issues faced universally such as kindness, selfishness and beauty coming from within. Children can investigate how the plot and setting of Cinderella changes as it is translated into a different culture together with the universal elements of the Cinderella story. In the Slavic tale *Twelve Months* (included in *Hidden Tales from Eastern Europe* by Antonia Barber), there is no glass slipper or a Prince Charming and yet it is still considered to be a version of Cinderella. It contains a wicked stepmother, Marushka (Cinderella) who is beautiful and mistreated, good wins over evil, and a handsome young man who worked the travelling cider-press falls in love with Marushka, marries her and they live happily ever after. This would be an ideal text to compare with the Cinderella story, to discuss key elements and how many elements need to be present in order to say, 'Yes, this is indeed a version of Cinderella'.

Comparing different versions using literature Venn diagrams will encourage the children to focus on the similarities and differences in the setting, characterisation and plot of up to three different versions. This could be completed as a class using chart paper and sticky notes or in smaller groups. It will also provide opportunities for learning through exploratory talk, as children make sense of new ideas and understandings as they talk about the stories together and have the opportunity to listen to and value each others' views. The graphical representation will also help with the understanding and recall of the stories.

Spellbinding storytelling

Storytelling enables children to develop their knowledge of stories and how story language works, and enhances their confidence and identity. Research evidence suggests that engagement with storytelling from a young age will make a significant contribution to later educational achievement. Gordon Wells claims that stories help children to make sense of their linguistic experience and enables them to learn how their language works, as well as providing a framework within which children interpret their own behaviours:

> In this way, stories are woven into the tapestry of a child's representations, producing the patterns that give it significance. (Wells, 2009: 216)

Storytelling can be an excellent way of supporting children with English as an additional language. It is imperative to respect and value the culture of all children within the classroom and providing children with the opportunity to hear and tell traditional tales in their own language is a good starting point. It is also an ideal opportunity to raise the profile of different languages and cultures in the classroom and to celebrate the sharing of diverse cultural experiences and knowledge. Parents also have a wealth of experience and knowledge of their culture's stories and can be invited in to share tales. As Blackledge states:

> The active use of languages as a planned part of the usual curriculum will promote all children's understanding of cultural diversity; such an understanding can be enhanced in the multilingual primary classroom by making use of the stories children bring to school. (Blackledge, 1994: 57)

As a result children with English as an additional language may develop their self-esteem, confidence, cultural identity and sense of place in the community through the sharing of their oral stories and traditions. The repetitive nature of traditional tales and the strong narrative structure can support children in their learning of English by introducing them to the vocabulary, grammatical structure and rhythm and sounds in the language. The use of gestures, facial expression and body language within storytelling can enable meaning making and understanding, and exploring stories through drama and role-play offers the opportunity to share cultural diversity, experience and knowledge as well as encouraging the use of the mother tongue.

The teacher and child as storyteller

As a teacher it is important to model storytelling to the children. Children need to consider gestures, use of voice, facial expressions, and pace and pauses to build tension – and all these aspects need to be demonstrated. There are professional storytellers available but generally it is the classroom teacher who has this role. However, some teachers, especially those new to the profession, may feel reluctant and lack confidence with telling a story aloud with no written text to rely upon. Telling stories is something both teachers and children need to practise and polish in order to become successful and so below there are some suggestions and strategies for both teachers and children to help develop their storytelling voice.

Teacher as storyteller:

- Choose a story you really like so that the passion comes through.

- Gather all the facts and details together.

- Decide from these the elements you are going to include and anything extra you wish to include.

- Note down the sequence of the story.

- Decide how you are going to begin the story.

- Visualise the start precisely.

- Develop your own voice by setting the scene.

- Involve the audience – this gives you thinking time before telling the next part of the story.

- Do not worry if you miss something out or add something extra in – this is what will make the story your own.

- Have faith in your own inventiveness.

Children as storytellers:

- Children could use prompts such as gold and silver coins and a small blue jug for the retelling of *The Persian Cinderella*.

- The use of puppets, masks, illustrations and photographs can aid storytelling.

- Story sacks or boxes containing simple artefacts from the tale will enrich and support the retelling.

- Start children off with a small audience – telling a story to a partner.

Children (and teachers) may require some support in enriching their memory of the plot and structure of a story in preparation for a retelling. The following strategies may be useful:

- *Story hands*. Children can draw around their hands and each finger can be used for a simple picture/word/phrase to act as prompts to retell the story.

- *Story plates*. Paper plates can be used to illustrate the sequences and main points of the story. *The Dragon Prince*: *A Chinese Beauty and the Beast Tale* by Laurence Yep would be a good choice here. The Chinese culture and the serpent and dragon characters in the story would lend themselves well to the story plate.

- *Story mountains*. The shape and size of mountains are used here to give a visual representation of the story structure. Pictures, symbols and words can be drawn on the mountains together with the high and low points of the story. This strategy works particularly well with climactic stories. The West African Folk Tale *Chinye* by Obi Onyefulu has a clear structure which would be ideal for this activity.

Using traditional tales as a stimulus for drama

Drama provokes children's imaginations and is an excellent way of promoting learning. While performance drama has its value in activities such as improvising with puppets, class performances in assemblies and school theatre productions, the most valuable drama for learning is that of process drama (O'Neill, 1995). This is also known as story drama (Booth, 1994) and classroom drama (Cremin, 2009). Classroom drama encourages children to explore issues in role and to work alongside the teacher who is also in role. Children are not asked to re-enact a story by performing a known tale but are asked to take the role of different characters from a range of cultures, wander into the world of others, learn from the stories and as a result gain a little insight into the tale and their own lives. It is the improvisational nature of classroom drama which challenges children to make up new narratives and to develop imaginative ideas as well as responding to those of others. As such, drama enables children to further develop their understanding of the tales, to question some of the issues within them and to develop new scenarios, understandings and meanings.

Moments within the tales can be chosen to explore themes, characters, conflicts, misunderstandings and different points of view. If the teacher tells the tale rather than reading it there is more opportunity to become a creative narrator as the story develops and the children's ideas can be woven into the tale as the drama progresses. When using classroom drama with traditional tales as a stimulus, it is better that the tales are unknown to the children otherwise they may be tempted to re-enact them. So the following activities need to be carried out before any work is conducted on comparison of tales, characters and storytelling.

Ideas for drama using *The Rough-Face Girl*

- Examine the front cover and generate possibilities about the tale and the culture.

- Make connections to other tales and known stories from this culture.

- As the two sisters march through the village children can 'become' the village people.

- Drawing in role – children could draw their own ideas of what the bow and runner of the sled are made of before they are revealed.

- Overheard conversations – what did the 'Invisible Being' hear the two sisters saying through the night? The children can be encouraged to consider the two girls' worries, fears, secrets, ideas and views.

- Hot seating of the father after he has given the Rough-Face Girl the shells and old moccasins.

- Group improvisation – in groups, one child to be the 'Rough-Face Girl' as she flaps through the village in the old moccasins; rest of the group to be the villagers, pointing at her and jeering.

- Flashback/flash forward – the tale does not revisit the sisters and father at the end. Children could conjecture and role-play what is happening to them after the Rough-Face Girl and the Invisible Being are married.

Ideas for drama using *The Three Rival Brothers*

The Three Rival Brothers (in *African Myths and Folk Tales* by Carter Godwin Woodson) has excellent opportunities for role-play. The three brothers are all vying for the hand in marriage of the chief's daughter and each has a different magical object. One has a glass which allows him to see far off places. The second brother has a hammock that can take whoever is sitting in it anywhere. The third has some medicine which can cure someone even if they are dead as long as the person has not been dead for more than three days. The three brothers use the magical objects to find out that the chief's daughter has died, to travel to her side and to cure her. The chief and the brothers cannot decide which of them is to marry the daughter. The tale ends not with a resolution but with the question, 'To which one of the brothers did the daughter belong?'

The story can be used as a stimulus for the role-playing of a court scene to decide who marries the daughter, with groups of children defending each of the three brothers. The children would need to mind map their reasons for why their brother should win the chief's daughter, decide which of the reasons would present the best case and develop a coherent and convincing argument. A child or the teacher could role-play a judge who presides over the proceedings. In the story, the voice of the daughter is not heard and the court case could be an opportunity for her point of view to be heard and indeed she may even be allowed to choose her husband herself!

Cinderella and cross-curricular links

Using traditional tales from across the world can provide excellent opportunities for cross-curricular work. As Barnes states, 'Our experience of the world is cross-curricular. Everything which surrounds us in the physical world can be seen and understood from multiple perspectives' (Barnes, 2007: 1).

Obvious examples of cross-curricular work include locating the countries on a globe or atlas and researching aspects of the culture and traditions. There are also many opportunities for artwork including Islamic patterns inspired from *The Persian Cinderella*, or lanterns could be made using items in the Chinese version, *Yeh-Shen*. Story quilts can be made using symbols from the story as the border and illustrations depicting the story in the sections.

There are often opportunities to include music and dance when exploring traditional tales. Retellings of the stories could include musical accompaniments such as drums for *The Rough-Face Girl* and bells for *Yeh-Shen*. Most Caribbean folk tales originate from Africa, where storytelling often included chanting, singing and dancing. There are some lovely examples of Caribbean traditional tales and music and dances to accompany them in *Sing Me a Story: Song-and-Dance Tales from the Caribbean* by Grace Hallworth. *Cendrillon* by Robert D. San Souci, a Caribbean Cinderella story, ends with a gwo-kā, a lively dance accompanied by drums, which children could choreograph and compose themselves.

Stephen Sondheim and James Lapine used the Brothers Grimm version of Cinderella in their musical *Into the Woods*. The Prologue of this musical is written in the style of a madrigal which is where three or more singers interweave lines, phrases and tunes to make new lines. Children can listen and watch parts of the prologue (which is available on the Internet) to observe the style of the songs. In small groups of three or four they can then create their own madrigal.

Conclusion

Stories are all around us and are a vital part of our lives. Traditional tales hold a special place in every child's cultural history and are a valuable resource for teaching and learning. They deal with issues such as love and hate and good and evil and other aspects of human experience which children will experience as they grow up. They can contribute to a child's emotional development and children easily make connections between their own lives and the stories they hear. The oral nature of traditional tales makes them memorable and ideal for storytelling, helping to develop children's knowledge and understanding of oral language. The gaps in the texts make them ideal for drama activities, developing children's understanding of and response to texts and cultivating skills such as inference and deduction. Traditional tales exist all over the world reinforcing the cultural identity of those who retell them. But more than anything, such tales capture the imagination of children and adults alike and we need to ensure that our children enjoy and pass on these wonderful tales to the next generation.

Something to read

South and North, East and West edited by Michael Rosen and published by Walker books includes some lovely tales from around the world, many of which have been collected from children in London.

See also the Society for storytelling website at: http://www.sfs.org.uk/.

Something to think about

This chapter has focused on the speaking and listening aspects of literacy learning. Consider the important link between oral language and writing and think of ways the use of traditional tales, storytelling and drama could impact upon children's writing and how lessons may progress into children structuring their own traditional tales.

Something to try

Investigate some of the myths from around the world with children. Geraldine McCaughrean has published a delightful version of the epic of Gilgamesh entitled *Gilgamesh the Hero: The Oldest Story Ever Told* which could be shared with older children.

If you have the opportunity to see a production of *Into the Woods* then do so – but don't expect a happy ending.

References

Barnes, J. (2007) *Cross-Curricular Learning 3–14*. London: Sage.

Bearne, E. (1994) 'Where do stories come from?', in M. Styles, E. Bearne and V. Watson (eds), *The Prose and the Passion*. London: Cassell.

Bettleheim, B. (1991) *The Uses of Enchantment: The Meaning and Importance of Fairy Tales*. London: Penguin.

Blackledge, A. (1994) '"We can't tell our stories in English": language, story and culture in the primary school', in A. Blackledge (ed.), *Teaching Bilingual Children*. Stoke-on-Trent: Trentham Books.

Booth, D. (1994) *Story Drama: Reading, Writing and Role-playing Across the Curriculum*. Ontario: Pembroke Publishers.

Cremin, T. (2009) *Teaching English Creatively*. London: Routledge.

Goodwin, P. (2008) *Understanding Children's Books: A Guide for Educational Professionals*. London: Sage.

Grainger, T. (1997) *Traditional Storytelling*. Rugby: Scholastic.

McCaughrean, G. (2002) *Gilgamesh the Hero: The Oldest Story Ever Told*. Oxford: Oxford University Press.

O'Neill, C. (1995) *Drama Worlds: A Framework for Process Drama*. Portsmouth, NH: Heinemann.

Rosen, M. (ed.) (2007) *South and North, East and West: 25 Stories from Around the World*. London: Walker Books.

Wells, G. (2009) *The Meaning Makers: Learning to Talk and Talking to Learn*. Bristol: Multilingual Matters.

Children's books mentioned in this chapter

Hans Christian Anderson, *The Snow Queen*. Andersen.

Antonia Barber, *Hidden Tales from Eastern Europe*. Frances Lincoln.

Shirley Climo, *The Persian Cinderella*. HarperCollins.

Grace Hallworth, *Sing Me a Story: Song-and-Dance Tales from the Caribbean*. Frances Lincoln.

Ai-Ling Louie, *Yeh-Shen: A Cinderella Story from China*. Philomel Books.

Rafe Martin, *The Rough-Face Girl*. Puffin Books.

Obi Onyefulu, *Chinye*. Frances Lincoln.
Charles Perrault, *Cinderella*. NorthSouth.
John Steptoe, *Mufaro's Beautiful Daughters*. Puffin Books.
Carter Godwin Woodson, *African Myths and Folk Tales*. Dover Publications.
Robert D. San Souci, *Cendrillon*. Aladdin Paperbacks.
Oscar Wilde, *The Happy Prince*. Orchard Paperbacks.
Laurence Yep, *The Dragon Prince: A Chinese Beauty and the Beast Tale*. HarperCollins.

Writing from experience

Justine Earl

Chapter Overview

This chapter explores ways to support children as they develop as writers. Although many of the suggested ideas are linked with the fiction genre, I hope to promote the idea that the writer's voice needs to be more important than the form of the text. While it is helpful to teach particular text types, this can be balanced with providing dedicated time which allows the young writer to develop their own ideas for their work. The child can also select the appropriate text type to be the vehicle for their chosen content. These are the decisions that real writers make all the time. The chapter offers ideas which allow children's voices to be heard through their writing. It challenges teachers to create a writing classroom which offers children authentic writing experiences and provides opportunities for writing which deals with children's thoughts, feelings issues and dilemmas. It hopes to move away from the apparently simplistic and formulaic approach where pupils succeed if they reproduce a given genre filled with language features from a predetermined and teacher-controlled list.

Approaches to writing: teaching a specific genre

Since the inception of the National Literacy Strategy (NLS) (1998), teaching writing in English classrooms has focused mainly on individual genre or text types within fiction, non-fiction and poetry. This continued as the NLS became the Primary National Strategy (PNS) (DfES, 2006) with the literacy units of work offering genre-based plans to follow. It could be said that organising the teaching of writing around the key features of given text types makes it more manageable for pupils and teachers. Focusing on one form – whether it is the traditional tale, science fiction, argument texts or humorous verse – allows the aims, success criteria and the final product to be very clear.

The use of genre theory in this way in the primary school context stems from a functional approach to languages (we learn language by using it), conceived by Michael Halliday (1975, 1978, 1985). Halliday's work influenced primary education, especially in Australia in the 1980s onwards. Here the genre tradition as represented by Martin (1985) aimed to allow all pupils to be educated in forms of writing which would enable them to function in society. This was an attempt to reconceptualise the teaching of writing.

The genre approach allows the teaching of writing to follow a clear structure at all levels. For example, the structure of the whole text can be set out, with the features of the text to be included at different points clearly indicated. For some texts this can be supported by writing frames, with useful sentence and paragraph starters. The actual teaching of the genre can also follow a clear structure, as follows:

- offer examples of the text type;

- analyse it;

- model it for the pupils via demonstration writing;

- scaffold the writing through supported and guided writing;

- present the final draft.

In this way, the structure, layout, features, grammar, style and register (level of formality) of a particular text type (be it a traditional tale, report, recount or argument text) can be shared, modelled and copied.

For many reasons, this can be a useful approach to teaching writing and you will find good ideas for specific genre work in this book. It allows a form to be understood before being tried out. Adult writers required to produce a work report for the first time would usually like to see an example so that they have some idea of what is required. It is not possible to write a haiku if we have not met one before and worked out the number of lines needed as well as the number of syllables in each line.

So, some benefits of using the genre approach to writing are the following:

- each genre or text type can be introduced separately, allowing a clear focus for a unit of work;

- specific features of the genre can be analysed and taught explicitly;

- the teacher is able to model the text type – providing a framework which pupils can use to develop their writing;

- supports can be offered, for example writing frames;

- text types can be used across the curriculum.

However, there are inherent dangers if this approach to teaching writing is not thought about carefully. Children may become over-reliant on a formulaic approach to text production, only able to achieve a complete piece of writing if frameworks are provided. If the children work only on a given text type because that is the focus of the current unit, the voice of each individual writer may be stifled. If as a pupil you are spending three weeks learning to write instructions then you may well master that text type. But what if during that time you are desperate to write a poem or a short story? The whole approach is very much teacher controlled, with the adult making the decisions in terms of what is to be written about and how.

Once a genre has been mastered, it can be recalled and reused in a new context. However, this is only guaranteed if a good teacher makes specific links between literacy units as well as between literacy and other subject areas. If, in literacy, you have been taught how to write a good recount, you may not think to put that knowledge into practice when asked to write about the invasion of Britain by Julius Caesar in 55 BC unless your teacher returns to the recount lesson and encourages you to draw on that knowledge and understanding. This is even trickier in schools where pupils are organised into sets for their literacy sessions.

So, some disadvantages of the genre approach are the following:

• teaching could become routine – leading to formulaic writing;

• there is often no clear purpose for the writing beyond reproducing the text type;

• pupils may become over-reliant on the supports offered;

• the process is very much teacher controlled; there is limited choice involved for the pupils;

• experience with the genre in a range of contexts may not be built effectively into the curriculum, leading to disconnected teaching and learning.

So which genre should be taught? When certain text types are suggested in national policy such as the PNS, it is easy for teachers to forget that these are not statutory. In fact, there is no prescribed list of genres that is compulsory for all children to experience. Of course, it is necessary to teach them a range of texts in fiction, poetry and non-fiction. Indeed, this book supports the teaching of many different texts types. However, since the introduction of the NLS and PNS, many teachers have accepted the suggested genre range without question. It is not certain that the range of texts offered even comes close to the current literacy experiences of the children in our classes. What of the texts which combine image and words and perhaps sound in a multimodal form? Children of today work comfortably with screen-based as well as paper-based texts.

Although it would be foolish to ignore the benefits of working with text types in order to understand and use them in the classroom and beyond, perhaps now is the time to revisit other options for the teaching of writing. By making possible the integration of other approaches and strategies, children can feel like real writers, whose voices and ideas matter more than the structures and forms of a text.

Approaches to writing: focusing on the process

How do pupils find their voice when writing in order to be able to play with genre, to communicate what they really want to say, to know what type of text is best for them at any one time? To do this, I believe we need to look once more at the process approach to writing, as championed by writers and researchers such as Frank Smith (1982, 1983, 1988), Donald Graves (1983, 1990, 1991) and Lucy McCormick Calkins (1986).

The process approach was developed in the 1980s and prioritises the context for the writing, with the creation of authentic texts with real purposes and audiences at its heart. Meaning and content are highly valued, with the child being seen as a real writer. Transcriptional aspects such as handwriting, spelling and grammatical issues are not ignored, but the main aim is for the teacher to aid composition and development of ideas.

Among the benefits of the process approach are the following:

- the writing experiences are authentic and meaningful, for real purposes and audiences;

- the writer's life, experiences, ideas and passions matter;

- response tends to be to the content and ideas rather than to the successful integration of predetermined features;

- transcriptional skills are learnt in a meaningful context;

- the teacher is a skilled partner in the work rather than having complete control over the writing.

Some criticisms of the process approach are as follows:

- the basic skills of grammar, handwriting and spelling are not taught sufficiently;

- children who are lacking in rich literacy experiences struggle;

- the approach does not take into account the need to be secure with certain text types as a vehicle for the writing in order for ideas to be communicated.

The next section will look at how integrating aspects of the process approach can be used to empower children as writers.

Children as writers

When children are urged to consider themselves as writers, they need to be helped to develop their own voice. This can be done by asking them to think about the following:

- what matters to them;

- how they can make use of their everyday experiences as inspiration for their writing;

- what forms they have at their disposal to express their planned content.

To start, children need to think about what they want to write. With fiction, all writers have potential ideas from their own lives and experiences, waiting for them to be recognised as a possible starting point. Of course, not all writing comes directly from a writer's experience, but many real authors do use their personal experiences as inspiration for their writing.

For example, the prolific children's writer Dick King Smith writes about animals because he spent twenty years as a farmer. Other significant authors who have used their own experiences, background or places important to them as part of their writing include C. S. Lewis, Philip Pullman, Beatrix Potter and Roald Dahl. Michael Morpurgo's entry on the British Council's contemporary writers' website states that he drew on his unhappy time at boarding school when writing *The Butterfly Lion*. The website also notes that:

> Morpurgo firmly believes that 'literature comes before literacy' and wants all children '... to discover and rediscover the secret pleasure that is reading, and to begin to find their voice in their own writing ...'

In my opinion, these are wise and helpful words.

Laura Summers' book *Desperate Measures* was shortlisted for the Waterstone's Children's book prize in 2010. She drew directly on her experience of bringing up a disabled child for this book. Many of the shortlisted books for 2010 dealt with tough issues for children, helping young readers to consider challenging subjects in a safe context. Such books, like those written by Jacqueline Wilson, offer texts which may inspire children to explore their own worries and concerns through their writing.

Autobiographical writing or writing from experience has rather lost its place in the primary classroom, often only being explored when it comes up as a specific unit of work. Yet for many writers, this is the first place to go to seek ideas and inspiration. As teachers we need to talk to children about where writers find their ideas – perhaps by inviting a 'real' writer into school – and how they might do the same. As Lucy McCormick Calkins writes: 'When we help children know that their lives do matter, we are teaching writing' (1986: 16).

In order to collect ideas for their writing, children might be helped to keep a writing notebook, rather like an artist's sketchbook, where embryonic ideas are kept and returned to. This might include words they have met and liked, or those they did not know the meaning of originally. Phrases and descriptions that they come across in books or other texts, including films and websites could be recorded as well as drawings and photographs which help them to visualise a particular setting, character or plot event. Clever endings, snippets of dialogue or text structures can be written down and returned to.

Lucy McCormick Calkins writes of her work with pupils and notebooks:

> I want children to know that this is a place to write, free from the eyes of a critical audience. I want the notebooks to encourage children to write about small, unimportant things, to explore a silly obsession, to carry on about their special interests, to explore private questions, to tell the truth. (McCormick Calkins, 1986: 120)

Of course, a writing notebook is also a place to record actual events in children's own lives: people they have met, things that have happened and problems with which they are struggling. In the research and development writing projects 'We're Writers' and 'Creativity and Writing' set up in schools in Kent in partnership with Canterbury Christ Church University, it was discovered that pupils wrote extensively outside school, including an extraordinary range of fiction, poetry and non-fiction texts. You can read about the work undertaken in developing children's writing voices in one of these projects in the book *Creativity and Writing: Developing Voice and Verve in the Classroom* (Grainger et al., 2005).

In some follow-up small-scale research (unpublished), the writing at home of four Key Stage 2 pupils was explored. I undertook this work with my colleague Teresa Cremin (previously Grainger) and presented some of our findings at a symposium entitled 'Diverse Voices: Text Construction at Home and School' for the UK Literacy Association 2007 conference. For me, the most striking aspect of this work was the highly individual and personal nature of the writing that the children did at home. The four pupils were all proficient writers and saw writing as part of their everyday lives. The texts they created at home did not relate to the genre being studied as part of their literacy work in school. The children did not worry about the transcriptional aspects, but they did enjoy deciding on their own form, layout and genre. They ranged from short, playful game-related texts to sustained story writing over a long period of time. They also included song lyrics, 'e-mail' exchanges written on paper to emulate a screen-based experience, play scripts and a series of related stories. Most importantly, what they wanted to say came first, then they made other choices such as form, layout, use of image, style and inclusion of colour. All of the texts they chose to talk about were paper-based, although all had some access to a home computer.

The out-of-school writing also dealt with issues that the young writers were struggling with to a greater or lesser extent – rehearsing difficult situations or dilemmas. For example, one girl wrote a poem entitled 'The Witch' about her dislike of the local shopkeeper and her fear of being sent on an errand to the shop:

> I feel like screaming when I get sent to the shops
>
> I know she will be there watching over me
>
> Is the watching good or bad, who can tell
>
> I know her voice like an old donkeys voice
>
> I know her breath like an old camels breath
>
> I know her hair like a horses tangled hair
>
> I know her nose like a rats tail
>
> I know her eyes like hawks eyes
>
> I know her pace like a tortoise pace
>
> I know her brain like a cheetahs brain
>
> Ready to pounce …

When talking about this poem, the eleven-year-old made it clear that actually she did not mind going to the shop as much as the poem suggests, but that taking an idea and exaggerating it in order to make a text is part of being a writer. She also wrote a sustained story about a family struggling with a disabled child which was inspired by her fascination with a documentary she had watched. Another pupil wrote about a recent family outing where she lost (and found again) her most beloved teddy bear, an incident on which she loosely based her writing, changing the details and settings as it suited her. It is possible that children write about what worries them because it puts that concern into some kind of manageable and safe context. They can explore their feelings in a way that is somehow under their control. They are even able to go some way towards resolving issues through their writing. As Ben Okri writes in his novel *Songs of Enchantment*: 'Stories can conquer fear, you know. They can make the heart bigger.'

Out of school writing is free from what the teacher wants, so it is truly the voice of the child. If a teacher is aware of the extent of the subjects that a child may choose to write about at home, this can be capitalised on in the classroom, avoiding young writers being given artificial tasks which expect them to replicate what the teacher has already offered as a model.

In 1996 Donald Graves wrote:

> I think many children are given assignments that force them to compose texts that have little to do with their own thoughts and feelings. It is practices like these that ensure that children will not be lifelong writers. That is, they won't use writing as a medium for thinking, for toying with ideas, in order to see more clearly what they think. (Graves, 1996: 11–12)

This was written before the advent of the NLS. I wonder if anything has changed.

There are practical things that can be done to continue to find, honour and develop the writer's voice into the later primary years. I have already mentioned the use of the writer's notebook for the collection of ideas. Some schools have introduced writing journals which give pupils a place to write whatever they wish in dedicated time in school. Sometimes these are taken home as well. Some teachers like to engage in a dialogue with their young writers in these books rather than marking them in the traditional sense. Other teachers do not look in them at all, regarding them as their pupils' private writing space. Using a writing journal means that even within a genre-based unit of work, there is somewhere for other types of writing to happen. For ideas on using writing journals try Lynda Graham's work for the UK Literacy Association.

To counter further the possible over-use of a genre-based literacy curriculum, time can be found on the timetable for the writing workshop. This is time outside the current study of a text type where all forms of writing are welcome and for all purposes. It can allow children to explore ideas, to take risks in their writing and to know that they will be listened to and supported – by their peers and by their teacher. By revisiting types of texts met so far in the term, children can be encouraged to try these out again, in new and perhaps unexpected ways. Pupils can bring in objects and photographs from home to help them to write. It might be a good time to consider things that really matter to the pupils as a starting point for ideas, either on a global, local or intensely personal scale. Lucy McCormick Calkins' (1986) book *The Art of Teaching Writing* provides excellent advice on writing workshops as well as on all aspects of working with young writers.

Here are some ideas for helping children to develop as writers:

- Ensure that your pupils are surrounded by good quality fiction, non-fiction and poetic texts as models of writing – continue reading aloud to the class as they progress through the primary years.

- Establish the use of writing notebooks to capture ideas.

- Encourage peer responses.

- Encourage collaborative writing.

- Use writing journals as a space for the child's choice of writing.

- With the children, analyse the genre that they are using in their journals.

- Demonstrate the value of their own experiences (however small).

- Find what it is that each child is passionate about.

- Include a regular writing workshop within your literacy timetable.

- Use children's own work as a basis for shared texts.

- Offer choice.

- Ensure that time is spent discussing the work with the children – as a class, in small groups and individually.

- Share your writing with the children – if as teachers we show the children that we too write, just as we often convince them that we are readers, then we will have a sense of shared endeavour.

Perhaps as teachers of writing we need to start by acknowledging that writing is in fact hard, messy and risky. At times it is unfinished. It can be difficult to assess. It can be short or long, wonderful or awful. It can lead to huge frustrations and great rewards. By offering an apparently simple answer to the children are we telling them the truth about writing? Maybe, as is often the case, the ideal way forward is a mixture of approaches. McCormick Calkins encourages her readers to spend significant chunks of the year working on a specific genre as a class, calling this part of the writing curriculum Genre Studies. She points out that this helps to prevent a young writer repeatedly writing in one form, as well as developing a sense of collaborative problem-solving as each genre is explored by the whole class. However, she warns against a set list of text types to study. She advocates offering her pupils examples of texts which she feels will 'evoke a powerful response' and then developing ways to allow them to 'live with the genre in whatever ways feel authentic, from doing choral readings and making anthologies of poems to reading picture books aloud to young children' (McCormick Calkins, 1986: 364). She also favours working with pupils to invent new ways of exploring genre. This way of working does not allow the routine and formulaic to dominate writing.

Conclusion

The ideas suggested in this chapter are not intended to replace completely your well established approaches to literacy. It is hoped that they will complement your work and fit with your already extensive knowledge of the children's abilities as writers, their targets and their writing National Curriculum levels. I would like any structured, formula-based/genre approach to be tempered by more opportunities for the creation of real texts which mean something to the children.

Teaching writing is hard. It requires us to listen to the children at every stage of the writing process, to consider how to help each child from beginning with a blank page to evaluating their published piece.

When I think about working with young writers I like to keep in mind these words from Lucy McCormick Calkins: 'Children need to be learners-of-writing more than they need to be producers-of-good writing'. I would like to think this is possible in the classrooms of today, despite the pressures of testing. I hope that the development of lifelong writers who feel that they have something to say and a voice to say it with is as important in your classroom as the making of pupils who know how to write a good SATs piece. I believe that a balance of structured genre work and the process approach can result in authentic pieces which matter to the children as well as writing which exceeds national expectations.

I agree with Wendy Body who wrote: 'The schools who treat children as writers and value both process and product are the schools who are likely to produce the children who relish writing and tackle it with great pride and enthusiasm' (Body, 1996). Can we ask for more than this?

Something to read

Many of the texts used in this chapter are quite old. I have chosen them deliberately. They are texts which have supported me in my own teaching of writing, sometimes reinvigorating me when I have lost my way somewhat with the pressure of levels, targets and SATs. Work through Donald Graves' *Build a Literate Classroom* (1991) trying the activities he suggests. This works very well if you can find a colleague to work with you and to compare ideas and results. Lucy McCormick Calkins' book *The Art of Teaching Writing* (1986) can also be used to reflect on your practice and to experiment with some of her ideas. I have found this book to be a real inspiration. Michael Rosen's invaluable book *Did I Hear You Write?* (1998) offers advice on working with pupils on what they really want to write about. He is a firm believer in honouring the voice of the child and tapping into what they already know.

Something to think about

What do you know about the writing your pupils do out of school? Consider asking the children in your class to log *any* writing which they do at home over a period of 2–4 weeks, so that you can understand more about them as writers and so make better connections with their in-school literacy.

Something to try

Become a writer. You might like to start by reading the chapter on teachers as artists in *Creativity and Writing* (Grainger et al., 2005). This describes the experiences of group members in the research project 'We're Writers' I talked about earlier. Tell your class that you are going to try and write something for them and talk to them about your progress. Share your challenges and successes with them, reading your work to them as you go and asking for their feedback and suggestions. You might be surprised by the results.

References

Body, W. (1996) '"I like to make something with words ..." Writers and writing', in B. Neate (ed.), *Literacy Saves Lives*. Royston: UK Reading Association.

DfEE (1998) *The National Literacy Strategy Framework for Teaching*. London: DfEE.

DfES (2006) *Primary National Strategy: Primary Framework for Literacy and Mathematics*. Nottingham: DfES Publications.

Graham, L. and Johnson, A. (2003) *Children's Writing Journals*. Royston: UK Literacy Association.

Grainger, T., Goouch, K. and Lambirth, A. (2005) *Creativity and Writings: Developing Voice and Verve in the Classroom*. London and New York: Routledge.

Graves, D. (1983) *Writing: Teachers and Children at Work*. Portsmouth, NH: Heinemann.

Graves, D. (1990) *Discover Your Own Literacy*, The Reading/Writing Teacher's Companion Series. Portsmouth, NH: Heinemann.

Graves, D. (1991) *Build a Literate Classroom*, The Reading/Writing Teacher's Companion Series. Portsmouth, NH: Heinemann.

Graves, D. (1996) 'Let's help children write with authentic voices', in B. Neate (ed.), *Literacy Saves Lives*. Royston: UK Reading Association.

Halliday, M. A. K. (1975) *Learning How to Mean: Explorations in the Development of Language*. London: Arnold.

Halliday, M. A. K. (1978) *Language as a Social Semiotic: The Theoretical Interpretation of Language and Meaning*. London: Arnold.

Halliday, M. A. K. (1985) *An Introduction to Functional Grammar*. London: Arnold.

McCormick Calkins, L. (1986) *The Art of Teaching Writing*. Portsmouth, NH: Heinemann.

Martin, J. R. (1985) *Factual Writing: Exploring and Challenging Social Reality*. Geelong: Deakin University Press.

Rosen, M. (1998) *Did I Hear You Write?*, 2nd edn. Nottingham: Five Leaves.

Smith, F. (1982) *Writing and the Writer*. New York: Holt, Rinehart & Winston.

Smith, F. (1983) 'Reading like a writer', *Language Arts*, 60: 558–67.

Smith, F. (1988) *Joining the Literacy Club: Further Essays into Education*. Portsmouth, NH: Heinemann.

Fiction mentioned in the chapter

Morpurgo, M. (1996) *The Butterfly Lion*. London: Collins.

Okri, B. (1993) *Songs of Enchantment*. London: Jonathan Cape.

Summers, L. (2010) *Desperate Measures*. London: Piccadilly Press Ltd.

Section 2

Poetry

Playground games as a foundation for literacy lessons

Sue Hammond and Karen Vincent

Chapter Overview

The focus of this chapter is on providing opportunities in the classroom for children to pursue their delight in the musicality and playful potential of language by using their knowledge of playground games. We aim to suggest ways of building on children's spontaneous engagement in this form of language learning without robbing them of their enjoyment or ownership of the form. However, it does have to be acknowledged that this is a danger and that part of the pleasure of playground rhymes and games may be related to the fact that they are beyond adult control and can be subversive or risqué or just plain silly! Rather than hijacking children's informal culture, the emphasis here is on valuing it and valuing the literacy practices that children from different socio-cultural backgrounds bring to their induction into school literacy and the practices of the dominant culture (Brice Heath, 1983; Grainger, 2004; Marsh and Hallet, 2008). The chapter is structured in the following way:

- What are the playground games, narratives and rhymes that children are currently engaging in? Why are they important to children's literacy learning?
- How can teachers use this knowledge? We begin this section with a case study and then provide more general suggestions for utilising and transforming the children's play ideas.

What playground games do children engage in and what is their significance for young children's literacy learning?

Play is widely recognised as the fundamental way in which children learn in their early years (David, 1996; Bruce, 2001; Moyles, 2005; Nutbrown, 2006). Indeed, it continues to be one of the essential modes through which we, as human beings, learn throughout our lives, although it is not always appreciated or given the status that it deserves. This is no less true of language acquisition than of other forms of learning. It has been suggested by linguists, such as Crystal (1998), Carter (2004) and Cook (2000), that a propensity to play with language is an innate part of the human condition. We love riddles and rhymes, jokes, puns and banter, limericks, tongue twisters, word play and games such as 'hangman', wordsearches, crosswords.

Everyday interactions and communications are littered with double entendres and language rule-bending from the banter of the binmen to the headlines written by subeditors in popular newspapers to the musings of philosophers.

Rhymes, songs and music are inextricably linked in the world of the young child, from the soothing lullaby sung to the youngest child, to the rhymes that familiarise children with each of their toes like 'This little piggy' and 'Baa, baa black sheep'. Both parties involved enjoy each of these forms of poetry. They allow opportunities for sharing, enjoyment and prediction, all necessary in the development of early reading skills. Music, songs and rhyme have an important place in children's learning experiences because they allow opportunities for active involvement and for tangible associations to form between a word and an action or object.

For young children, their most natural form of expression is movement, and songs and rhymes enable total physical involvement and immersion in this process. Allowing them the freedom to express themselves has firm links with cognitive development, linguistic development and social development. Research (e.g. Bradley and Bryant, 1991) has shown that familiarity with rhyme early on can also lead to later reading success. 'Studies show a very strong relationship between rhyming ability at age three and performance at reading and spelling three years later. A number of studies have reinforced the value of such early exposure to rhyming games' (see http://ezinearticles.com/?Teach-Your-Child-Phonemic-Awareness&id=209419). Children naturally continue to engage with rhyme and rhythm as they enter the world of the school playground. Here, they encounter children of different ages enjoying spontaneous exchanges with each other in the form of chants, songs and rhymes. Their curiosity leads them to learn more about the rules and systems in place if they are to share in this new world.

According to our male informants aged 7, 9 and 10 years, their playground games in 2010 include 'chase, it, hide and seek, catch, leap frog, bulldog, stuck in the mud, football along with some chanting games', with skipping games tending to be the girls' territory. While this gender divide resonates with the research findings of Pellegrini et al. (2004), of more relevance here is the rich potential of games, songs and rhymes for the literacy curriculum. The most widely known and comprehensive study of children's playground lore to date was that conducted by Iona and Peter Opie in the 1950s. Among their records are examples of nonsense rhymes, parodies, skipping and satirical rhymes, and of chase, hide and seek games, at the heart of which there is often a rhythmic or repetitive chant or phrase.

This is the stuff of poetry writing: the games and rhymes provide the frame, and the playground provides the space where children are able to develop, rehearse and express their poetic voices in a 'safe' and meaningful way. They are immersed in the cadences, sounds and structures of language, often within the context of traditional narratives and archaic words, and experiment with beats, rhythms, silences and pauses. They are engrossed in memorisation, experimentation and enjoyment. In their playground games they have the opportunity to 'play around' with language and ideas – freely, spontaneously, often subversively – without being constrained by adult rules or sanctions. The texts and songs that children rehearse, construct and own in these contexts are powerful texts.

Indeed, Michael Rosen, who is a passionate spokesperson for children's right to rich language and literature experiences, rails against an education system where, 'Kids don't get the chance to get up and perform poetry, and enjoy it, because they're too busy counting adjectives and spotting metaphors' (Rosen, 2009). Yet young children are deeply involved in just such performances in the playground, particularly in skipping, jumping and clapping games. Wonderfully rich examples of these can be seen not only in the playground but on school websites or in videos on the Internet where children are joyously engaged in their own localised versions of the rhymes and want to share them with the world! Although in our primary schools, we have to be conscious of Internet safety, children can be involved in creating a website archive or videoing and producing a DVD for other classes and for families, taking ownership of their learning.

A focus on playground traditions can be an ideal route for bridging the gap between home and school because it provides a context for conversations, sharing experiences and building relationships. For those parents whose memories of school are not positive ones, playground life may be a more neutral domain and provoke happier recollections. The authors of this chapter have both involved parents and grandparents in the class topics they have undertaken on playground games. As well as bringing different generations and groups of people together, such projects are a means of preserving long-standing traditions and give the children the chance to induct their families and teachers into their own games, songs and rhymes so that everyone's repertoires are enhanced and appreciated.

Amid fears that children's lives are becoming more sedentary and that playground lore is dying out (Kenny, 2009), a literacy project that starts with children's everyday activities seems an ideal way of redressing the balance. Physical skipping or clapping rhymes can help to develop gross motor skills, encourage exercise, develop stamina and help with coordination. Some skipping rhymes are quite complex necessitating the ability to sing, clap and think of a chain of related words all at the same time! Playground rhymes can help to boost cooperation and teamwork in the playground. Nevertheless, there is often ambivalence in adults' attitudes towards children's play, not least in their concerns about the apparently violent nature of boys' playground games or the prevalence of fantasy play based on superheroes or other popular culture. Among recent comments from student teachers and teaching assistants were complaints that children in Reception and Year 1 classes 'did not know any games they could play in the playground. As a result they ended up fighting or being aggressive and ... made up their own imaginary games ... Myself and the teacher then went out at playtime with the children and had to teach them games ...'; 'only played Ben Ten' (a popular television programme) or 'dogs'. We want to allay these concerns and suggest alternative interpretations of the games in addition to ideas for incorporating them into literacy learning in the classroom.

It may be disquieting to think that the youngest children in schools do not have a stock of playground games but *teaching* them 'Duck, duck, goose', 'Please Mr Crocodile', 'What's the time, Mr Wolf?' or 'He', 'Hokey Cokey', 'I sent a letter to my love', the 'Bean' game, etc., affords perfect opportunities for extending speaking and listening skills, developing coordination and collaboration and introducing textual composition. They also lend themselves to children making picture books or even digital pop-up storybooks[1] of the games, or taking photographs of the different elements of a game and writing instructions and rules.

Additionally, any of these activities could be used to capture the 'imaginary games' mentioned above so that the children's inventiveness and their prowess in working together gains recognition, rather than their own games being regarded simply as less acceptable. Concerns about boys' violent and aggressive behaviours are not always founded in fact (Jarvis, 2007) and there is often a concerted effort on the part of participants not to make actual contact when they are engaged in fighting or other forms of rough and tumble play. Furthermore, there are *child* rules and sanctions (Pellegrini et al., 2004) to be adhered to and the rules of a peer group can be more rigorous and exacting than those of the grown-ups.

A friend who teaches a Year 1 class decided to exploit the children's enthusiasm for certain television programmes and has successfully incorporated their fascination with musical dramas and superheroes, including 'Ben Ten', into her language and literacy planning. The children produce their own plays and playscripts, design scenery and costumes, or make puppets. They then create tickets, posters and programmes for their performances; another class in the school attends the dress rehearsal and the final show is staged for parents and grandparents. Their narratives are drawn from the socio-dramatic play they have engaged in during their playground adventures and although they are influenced by the events and characterisations of the television dramatisations, they are not mere re-enactments. Just as most authors do, the children extract ideas from a range of texts and experiences and transform the stories in their own versions. Although the use of popular culture in the classroom has its critics and is often denigrated, it seems perverse of teachers not to use children's existing knowledge and interests as a platform for developing literacy skills.

It does have to be acknowledged, nevertheless, that the playground is an unhappy space for some young children and they may struggle to find the words or the confidence to communicate their distress or loneliness. However, carefully managed literacy opportunities can create the environment for sharing this information. Pahl (2008) describes the drawings and speech bubbles that were the context for one young child to convey her unpleasant associations with playtimes. Although this was not the intention in the project that Pahl refers to, a text like this can be a means for enabling the child's voice to emerge and for teachers to find ways of overcoming the isolation that the child is feeling.

A case study

In the second part of this chapter, Karen, one of the authors of this chapter, shows, through a case study, how a specific unit of work grew from a wider topic and was underpinned by the views outlined so far. It afforded powerful language and literacy experiences as well as providing meaningful cross-curricular opportunities for teaching and learning.

The setting for this classroom work was a medium-sized primary school in an 'urban village' on the outskirts of a town in south-east England. The school benefits from being situated in beautiful grounds with spectacular views over the Weald of Kent. The stepped site contains three large playgrounds and a tiered field on two levels. The school is fortunate to have wooden play apparatus, a quiet area and a nature reserve complete with viewing deck funded by a supportive PTA who value the outdoor environment and the contribution it makes to learning. The overarching topic was based on the theme of 'Our Local Area' and involved a Year 1 class in exploring various places such as the church, the shops and the woods. Each of these places had wider connections with other curriculum areas. For example, the visit to the church enabled a clearer understanding of both the history and purpose of the building as well as the functions of its internal and external fixtures. The shops provided opportunities to make important decisions about which sweets could be bought for 10p and what change would be required as well as reflections on the route taken and the features along the way. The woods provided a unique, evocative environment in which to study mini beasts and plants as well as the opportunity to role-play 'We're going on a bear hunt!'

Within this wider context, the focus was specifically upon a study of the school and the areas used at playtimes. The children were provided with clipboards or notebooks for a tour of the school so that they could note various features and their purposes, for example drainpipes and pathways and where they led. Listening skills were enhanced when the children crouched quietly in the nature reserve to see and hear what creatures were there. The task of redesigning the playground and making models to show new and improved features required language and communication skills and a range of other cognitive and physical skills.

This naturally led to a focus on the games the children enjoyed playing during playtimes and, with limited resources outside, there were many imaginative ideas to share. One of the themes that came out of this discussion was the wealth of rhymes that children engaged in while playing, both in the playground and on the field, which encompassed all sorts of skipping, clapping and chanting rhymes. The children were very motivated and excited at the prospect of sharing rhymes and games with the rest of the class. High levels of motivation in recalling the rhymes were clear to see because the children had ownership of their activities during playtime. It was an opportunity for them to develop their social skills and work together. Pellegrini and Blatchford (2002) have described this time as a 'natural laboratory': a time when students of a variety of ages can interact with each other on their own terms with minimal adult interference. Playtimes are not always valued for their educational value but by utilising and capturing the high levels of motivation that children display when engaging in rhymes, songs and chants in the playground, it is possible to engage them in literacy activities inside and outside the classroom.

As part of the topic, the parents of the children in the class were asked to recall what games they had enjoyed in the playground as children. The objective here was for the children in the class to begin to appreciate that generations past enjoyed playground rhymes as much as they did. These children in the past included their own parents and grandparents. Many parents and family members wrote down the rhymes that they remembered. Some taught the children the rhymes and the children in turn taught others at school.

It became clear that some of the playground rhymes that their parents shared were the same as, or very similar to, the rhymes that the children in the class were familiar with. Some were traditional favourites like 'London's Burning', 'One Potato, Two Potato' and 'Oranges and Lemons'. Others, like 'Ippy, dippy, dation, my operation, how many people at the station?' were new to the children. The rhymes were categorised into clapping, skipping and choosing rhymes by the children (see below) and great fun was had in trying them out both in the classroom and in the playground during PE and Literacy sessions.

Clapping

> A sailor went to sea, sea, sea,
>
> To see what he could see, see, see.
>
> But all that he could see, see, see,
>
> Was the bottom of the deep, blue sea, sea, sea.

Skipping

Two people skipping with one shared rope recite:

> Mummy's in the kitchen,
>
> Doing a bit of stitchin',
>
> In came a burglar and Mummy ran OUT.

(On the word 'out' the 'burglar' replaces the child who has run out in time to sing the song again.)

> Cinderella, dressed in yellow, went upstairs to kiss her fella, how many kisses did she get? One, two, three, four, five, etc.
>
> All in together girls,
>
> Never mind the weather girls,
>
> Please jump in on your birthday.

(Jump in on your birthday month until all in and then say it again and jump out on your birthday month.)

> January, February, March, April, etc.
>
> Inky, Pinky, Ponky,
>
> Daddy met a donkey,
>
> Donkey died,
>
> Daddy cried,
>
> Inky, Pinky, Ponky.

Choosing

> Eeny, meeny, miny, mo,
>
> Catch a monkey by its toe,
>
> If it hollers let it go,
>
> Eeny, meeny, miny, mo.
>
> Ip, dip, do,
>
> Cat's got the flu,
>
> Dog's got the chickenpox,
>
> So out goes you.

After the rhymes had been categorised according to their purpose in the playground (clapping rhymes to learn a set sequence of claps in time to the beat, skipping rhymes to be performed with a rope and choosing rhymes in order to decide on which child would be 'it' for example) and shared with others in the class, the process of transforming the rhymes within the classroom could begin. In the next section we will discuss how these rhymes were used within a classroom-based context and transformed to fulfil National Curriculum objectives.

Utilising and transforming the children's play ideas

This part of the chapter shows some examples of how the initial immersion into popular playground culture transformed into classroom-based activities and addressed the following National Curriculum objectives:

- Group discussion and interaction (English 1 Speaking and Listening, 3a, 3b, 3d).

- Reciting and learning poems with patterned and predictable language (English 2 Reading, 6e).

- Linking sound and letter patterns, exploring rhyme, alliteration and other sound patterns (English 2 Reading, 1h).

- Identifying patterns of rhythm, rhyme and sounds in poems and their effects (English 2 Reading, 3e).

- Use their voices effectively by singing songs and speaking chants and rhymes (Music KS1, 1a).

- Rehearse and perform with others (Music KS1, 1c).

- Identify different ways in which the past is represented (History KS1, 3).

There were also many other benefits to starting with the children's popular playground culture. It was fun and it gave them all a voice. They all contributed to the topic in their individual ways and it enabled children with different cultural backgrounds to share their songs, rhymes and poems. For children with English as an additional language, it gave them an opportunity to expand their vocabulary at the same time as reinforcing the language through repetition and actions. This helped them to embed their understanding of the language alongside their peers.

After many rhymes had been shared, we began to take ownership of them by transforming them using the children's ideas. This started with a teacher-led session where we transformed the words of a familiar rhyme and had the clock in 'Hickory Dickory Dock' strike two, three, four and five:

Hickory, dickory, dock, the mouse ran up the clock, the clock struck two, the mouse said 'boo', hickory, dickory dock.

Hickory, dickory, dock, the mouse ran up the clock, the clock struck three, the mouse went 'wee' (hand gestures as if on a roller coaster required!), hickory, dickory, dock.

Hickory, dickory dock, the mouse ran up the clock, the clock struck four, the mouse fell through the floor, hickory, dickory, dock.

Hickory, dickory, dock, the mouse ran up the clock, the clock struck five, the mouse did a jive, hickory, dickory, dock.

The children had enormous fun thinking of words that rhyme with each number. They had lots of ideas and because the teacher wanted them all to be involved, anything was accepted. The suggestions ranged from sensible substitutions to silly ones. Following this, we moved to transforming one of the playground rhymes. 'Inky, Pinky, Ponky' was a great favourite among the children and lent itself particularly well to word substitution. The children worked in pairs to think of a new animal instead of a donkey and about how that would transform the word 'ponky' in the rhyme. Ponky is a great word because it is nonsense and so any other letter substitution works equally well: a real bonus when working with young children and rhyme! Some transformed the poem into:

Inky, Pinky, Pog,

Daddy had a dog,

Dog died, Daddy cried,

Inky, Pinky, Pog.

Some children went on to transform their rhyme further by changing the character in the rhyme too. For example:

Inky, Pinky, Pat,

Mummy had a ... cat,

Cat died,

Mummy cried,

Inky, Pinky, Pat.

These ideas were then tried out on each other, being careful to pause before the end of the second line in order for others to guess what the animal might be. Further development included working out clapping rhythms to go with the poem. At their simplest, these were hands on lap, hands clap, then repeat as you recite the rhyme. Further levels of complexity included sitting opposite a partner to clap each other's hand both horizontally and crossed. Motivation levels were high and we felt particularly fulfilled when the children shared their newly composed playground games with others in the playground.

Revisiting the playground rhymes topic

A recent visit back to the class showed that many of the children still enjoyed singing some of the playground songs and rhymes that they learnt in their earlier days at the school. We shared some of these examples and tried hard to remember others together. There were flashes of recognition as some of the long forgotten rhymes re-entered their heads. I teased them by reading the beginning of the rhyme and then pausing to see if they could complete the end of the rhyme: 'Ippy, dippy, dation, my operation, how many people at the ... station.' They could! We tried another: 'Mummy's in the kitchen, doing a bit of ... (stitchin'), along came a burglar and Mummy ran OUT!' Yes, the rhymes that they once knew were coming back. I tried another. 'Cinderella, dressed in yellow, went upstairs to kiss a ... (fella), how many kisses did she get?' By now, most of the class were joining in with me and enjoying the experience. It was pleasing to discover that about a third of the children still sang this rhyme while skipping. It was the skipping rhymes that we ended up focusing on, largely because many of the children still enjoyed skipping and singing in the playground. They had built quite substantially on their repertoire since Year 1 and had some new ones to teach me!

It appears that children are very skilled at differentiating the skipping and clapping rhymes for themselves as they appear to get increasingly complex as they get older. For example, this clapping rhyme was performed in a circle by Year 5s and 6s:

Concentration, sixty-four,

Hesitation, is no more,

I'll go first, you'll go second ...

The subject is ... (any subject);

People in the class. (List them and stay in time to the beat!)

The complexities of remembering the words to the rhyme, pausing at the correct time and staying in time to the beat as well as thinking of a subject and/or making word associations in time is very demanding. For these reasons we should not discount the intrinsic, motivational value that playground rhymes, chants and songs can bring to the literacy curriculum. Persistence, failure and repetitiveness are all part of the process of rehearsal and improvement of any performance. The process of learning is hard but by giving children control of the subject content and valuing children's playground culture alongside carefully planned activities, a sense of learning together can be enjoyed. Let the children take the lead; they love to teach us things and share their own unique perspectives with us. It is up to us to listen and respond in respectful ways. By joining in with their rhymes, chants and rhythms, we can learn to respond to their beat and take their literacy learning forward in new and exciting directions.

Something to read

Beck, I. and King, S. (1985) *Oranges and Lemons: Singing and Dancing Games.* Oxford: Oxford University Press.

Clark, V. (1991) *High Low Dolly Pepper: Developing Music Skills with Young Children.* London: A&C Black.

Gardner, S. (1995) *Playtime Rhymes.* London: Orion Children's books.

Something to think about

What playground rhymes, songs or chants did you sing when you were at school? Are there any that the children in your class have not heard? Can you remember them well enough to teach the children in your class? Observe your current class and note the children's playground games, narratives and rhymes. This can provide a simple starting point for your planning and an important bridge between informal literacy experiences and the 'official' curriculum. You can extend this to community involvement by providing opportunities for parents and carers to add to your collections.

Something to try

Ask the children in your class what playground rhymes they know. Share your own rhymes and ask individuals to share theirs with the whole class or in smaller groups. For the next session, select one of these rhymes that would be suitable for transformation into a new rhyme. During the session, think about one of the words or characters that could be substituted by another. Organise the children into pairs or threes and ask them to think of some examples of words or characters (you could have a collection of picture prompts to offer if needed) that they can substitute so that they invent a new rhyme to share with the class.

Note

1 For details of creating a pop-up digital story book see: http://www.alpha.zooburst.com/.

References

Blatchford, P. (2003) 'The social context of school playground games: sex and ethnic differences and changes over time after entry to junior school', *British Journal of Developmental Psychology*, 21 (4): 481–505.

Bradley, L. and Bryant, P. (1991) 'Phonological skills before and after learning to read', in S. Brady and D. P. Shankweiler (eds), *Phonological Processes in Literacy*. Hillsdale, NJ: Erlbaum, pp. 37–45.

Brady, S. and Shankweiler, D. (eds) (1991) *Phonological Processes in Literacy. A Tribute to Isabelle Y Liberman*. Hillsdale, NJ: Laurence Erlbaum Associates.

Brice Heath, S. (1983) *Ways with Words: Language, Life and Work in Communities and Classrooms*. New York: Cambridge University Press.

Bruce, T. (2001) *Learning through Play: Babies, Toddlers and the Foundation Years*. London: Hodder & Stoughton.

Carter, R. (2004) *Language and Creativity: The Art of Common Talk*. London: Routledge.

Cook, G. (2000) *Language Play, Language Learning*. Oxford: Oxford University Press.

Crystal, D. (1998) *Language Play*. London: Penguin.

David, T. (1996) 'Their right to play', in C. Nutbrown (ed.), *Respectful Educators, Capable Learners: Children's Rights and Early Education*. London: Paul Chapman.

Factor, J. (2001) 'Three myths about children's folklore', in J. Bishop and M. Curtis (eds), *Play Today in the Primary School Playground*. Buckingham: Open University Press.

Grainger, T. (ed.) (2004) *The Routledge Falmer Reader in Language and Literacy*. London: RoutledgeFalmer.

Jarvis, P. (2007) 'Monsters, magic and Mr. Psycho: a biocultural approach to rough and tumble play in the early years of primary school', *Early Years*, 27 (2): 171–88.

Marsh, J. and Hallet, E. (eds) (2008) *Desirable Literacies: Approaches to Language and Literacy in the Early Years*. London: Sage.

Moyles, J. (ed.) (2005) *The Excellence of Play*. Maidenhead: Open University Press.

Nutbrown, C. (2006) *Threads of Thinking: Young Children Learning and the Role of Early Education*. London: Paul Chapman.

Opie, I. and Opie, P. (1951) *The Oxford Dictionary of Nursery Rhymes*. Oxford: Oxford University Press.

Opie, I. and Opie, P. (1959) *The Lore and Language of Schoolchildren*. Oxford: Oxford University Press.

Pahl, K. (2008) 'Looking with a different eye: creativity and literacy in the early years', in J. Marsh and E. Hallet (eds), *Desirable Literacies: Approaches to Language and Literacy in the Early Years*, 2nd edn. London: Sage. pp. 140–61.

Pellegrini, A. and Blatchford, P. (2002) 'The developmental and educational significance of recess in schools', *Early Report* (University of Minnesota), 29 (1): 1–7.

Pellegrini, A., Blatchford, P., Kato, K. and Baines, E. (2004) 'A short-term longitudinal study of children's playground games in primary school: implications for adjustment to school and social adjustment in the USA and the UK, *Social Development*, 13 (1): 107–23.

Wyse, D. and Jones, D. (2008) *Teaching English Language and Literacy*. London: Routledge.

Website references

Kenny, E. (2009) 'Fiona Phillips reveals how treasured childhood activities are dying out', online at: http://www.youtube.com/watch?v=zC65fjFIN58&feature=related. (Kenny, a psychologist, analysed the results of a survey of 4,000 parents by a soft drinks company.)

Mascle, D. Online at: http://ezinearticles.com/?Teach-Your-Child-Phonemic-Awareness&id=209419 (accessed 23 July 2010).

Rosen, M. (2009) 'Portrait of the artist: Michael Rosen', *Guardian*, Tuesday, 21 July, online at: http://www.michaelrosen.co.uk/.

5

Using poetic form: an approach to poetry writing in the primary classroom

Susan Barrett and Virginia Bower

Chapter Overview

This chapter will discuss what we consider to be a key aspect relating to the teaching of poetry and children's poetry writing in the primary classroom; that the explicit use of poetic forms is an important way to support children as they begin to write their own poems. We will first identify both the acknowledged strengths and weaknesses of this approach, referring to key writers in this field; we will then go on to discuss how poetic form can be used effectively in the primary classroom and suggest ways to avoid the possible pitfalls; finally 'real life' examples of classroom practice will be analysed, where existing poems were used to scaffold pupils' writing. This section will include examples of children's writing.

Engaging with a range of viewpoints relating to the use of form

Exploring and delighting in poetry is a vital element of everyday classroom practice. If children are encouraged to read and enjoy poems, when you then come to study poetic form in more depth, they will have a positive attitude towards, and a background knowledge and understanding of, this genre. The vast majority of children come to school with their heads already full of jingles, song lyrics, nursery rhymes and a predisposition towards playing with forms of language. As Margaret Meek (1991) discusses, through their play they already show a flair for metaphor when sticks become light sabres and empty boxes boats. The problem for teachers is deciding how to use this existing knowledge effectively and to balance it with the desire to introduce children to a range of poetic devices, forms, structures and language. There is a need to celebrate the freedom which a child can experience when composing their own poetry, promoting creativity and allowing them to develop their own unique voices through this form, while providing them with enough support to give them the confidence to believe in themselves as poets.

Anthony Wilson (2001) has summarised the methods offered by four key figures in the realm of supporting children's poetry writing: Sandy Brownjohn, Michael Rosen, Jill Pirrie and Ted Hughes. We shall look briefly at these methods, as they offer a range of perspectives which are important to consider when deciding on the best way to approach poetry writing in *your* classroom.

Brownjohn's approach (1994), which includes games to introduce metaphor easily and an emphasis on manipulating language freely but within a structure, allows children to focus at the micro-level of word or line. This, she claims, 'takes the pressure off' and so the child learns confidence in a range of techniques. Wilson (2001), an enthusiastic exponent of her approaches in his early teaching career, calls this the 'apprentices in workshop' model.

Michael Rosen, the current children's poet laureate, in contrast, thinks poetry writing should be linked less with the reading of poetry and more with the 'oral expression of the experience' (Rosen, 1998: 86). With his emphasis on developing children's pre-existing competence in oral language, he is not in favour of adults imposing what he considers to be an arbitrary notion of what literary forms are best:

> We need to find forms that release children's knowledge, liberate it and so give the child a sense of his or her own power. (1998: 41)

With his emphasis on 'oral writing', he promotes the idea of encouraging children to 'try and reproduce the feel of their inner speech on the page' (1998: 70). His concern about any 'technique' approach to poetry is, 'You end up with stuff that sounds great but in essence means very little to whoever wrote it' (1998: 72). Wilson sums up Rosen's approach as treating children as 'sentient individuals with something to say' (2001: 5) and who should be encouraged to find their own forms when writing.

Rosen's acknowledged irreverent approach to poetry is beguiling and played out consistently in his broadcasts, books, performances and work with schools. In direct contrast with this approach is Jill Pirrie's work (1987, 1994), which is rooted in the poetic forms of established poets. These she uses to enlarge the child's inner experience, imposing poetic form as a constraint 'in order to set free' the child writer. In this way, children are seen as 'conscious artists' (Wilson, 2001: 5) trying to establish mastery over their writing. The difficulty for Rosen with this approach is that it appears to favour certain poetic forms over others in a hierarchical way and reduces the ideas of what poetry might be. There is also the opinion that, if children are *constrained* by form, then they lose any chance of spontaneity and originality.

The final perspective to consider is that of Ted Hughes, that gloriously innovative poet who offers an amalgamation of some of the aforementioned ideas. He believes children should experience a wide range of poetry, but that which might be offered as a model should be characterised by 'basically plain, modern speech' (1963: 12). Those familiar with his work will not be surprised by the emphasis he places on the senses, but otherwise children should have 'many opportunities and few restraints'.

What do all these perspectives have to offer a busy classroom teacher, particularly one who may not be a subject specialist? While the approaches so far outlined might appear disparate, they all share a common purpose: to get children writing. Carter (1998: 18) suggests, 'Every poet who ever wrote owes a lasting debt to his or her favourite poets'. But does this 'scavenging' approach preclude the development of the child's voice as a writer? Carter would argue that this is not the case. When children use established poets as inspiration or as models, 'there is a sense in which they tease out strands of [Coleridge] and add strands of themselves to make something new' (1998: 92).

From our own research and classroom experience, although we recognise the possible pitfalls, we believe that using poetic forms as models on which children might base their writing is an effective strategy, providing care is taken that children do not neglect content because of an over-focus on form. By encouraging children to focus on the experience they want to write about and look at examples of poems by existing poets to inspire and motivate them, or by offering forms which are less technically demanding in rhyme and metre but still allow the young writers to shape experience (list poems, kennings and haiku for example), we are striving to maintain a balance between providing support while promoting freedom and creativity.

Using poetic form to support poetry writing

Schools have, in the past, perhaps overemphasised language, imagery and the poetic devices which support this when teaching poetry writing. This has not always enabled children to 'unlearn' some of the conventions of prose writing (continuous, punctuated and paragraphed and so on) to allow them to wrestle with the considerable cognitive demands of writing poetry and has often resulted in self-conscious over-use of figurative language, designed to fulfil what children understand to be the expectations of the teacher.

To avoid these dangers and pitfalls relating to the use of poetic form and to escape the possibility of your class producing thirty formulaic and very similar poems, here are some key points you might find useful:

- *Use high-quality literary models*. Children need to be exposed to and immersed in a wide range of high-quality poetic texts, allowing them to absorb the rhythms and cadences of different styles and forms of poems.

- *Combine exposure and immersion with personal experience*. Encourage children to use their own experiences within their writing and to find their own voice because of the very nature of these personal experiences. In this way, it is about *empowerment* more than *imitation*.

- *Foster and encourage interactive responses*. This can be promoted through drama, performance, art, music and so on, and lies at the heart of a unit of work on poetry, before any act of writing takes place.

- *Modelling, sharing, guiding*. It is vital not only to use existing poems as models for the children, but also to demonstrate the actual writing process by modelling it yourself. Modelled writing allows you to talk through each stage as you go, making mistakes, editing, rewriting, etc. and in this way children are given the confidence to 'have a go' themselves. This can lead to shared and collaborative writing, where the teacher can act as scribe, removing the onus of transcription and leaving the children free to contribute their ideas. Teacher modelling and collaborative, shared writing would allow the focus to move from language choices (still an important feature) to explicit discussion about structure, rhyme, rhythm, stanzas and so on. Wilson (2007: 445) in his work used 'explicit modelling from specific poems' and 'indirect modelling from a wider body of work' but they were used according to the developmental needs of his pupils and always with the understanding that children may want to create meanings of their own. When children then move on to their own compositions, guided writing sessions – working with one small group at a time – are vital to provide support where needed, whether that be intensive support with children who are just getting to grips with poetry writing or thinking of ways by which to extend the more able.

Some examples from practice

This section looks at how existing poems were used in our classrooms to inspire and support children with their own poetry writing. The first example is centred around the use of kenning poems.

Kennings are a particular poetic form, originally from Old Norse, which lend themselves to imitation, yet provide opportunities for children to focus at the micro-level (akin to Brownjohn's approach mentioned previously) on word combinations. A kenning poem uses compound phrases which describe an object metaphorically, i.e. a cat might be described as a 'mouse catcher' or a chair as a 'leg saver'. This particular form allows children the freedom to draw on their own knowledge and understanding of the world and personal experiences while having the support of a very clear structure.

The following poem was produced by a Year 5 pupil, having read Steve Turner's poem 'Sun':

Wrestler

Back-breaker

Risk-taker

Man-lifter

Body-shifter

Bone-grinder

Weapon-finder

Muscle-flexer

Move-mixer

Costume-wearer

Belt-sharer

Hair-puller

Microphone-yeller

This pupil who, ordinarily found writing a chore, was able to convey his fascination with wrestling – a passion he shared with his grandfather – gaining confidence from the 'tight' structure of this poetic form. Here he played with rhyme as well as creating powerful images from his frequent and close observation of this activity. 'Muscle-flexer', 'Costume-wearer' and 'Hair-puller' are all recognisably part of the created artifice of today's wrestling ring!

In preparation for writing this kenning poem, the child was immersed within the poetic form, through shared and guided reading and having the opportunity to access kennings independently. He was encouraged to make word lists relating to his field of interest before embarking on the writing of the poem. It might be argued that certain classroom practices mitigate against children's poetic voices developing. For example, compiling class lists of words or phrases may mean that they are 'caught within someone else's agenda. The children will give back what they think is expected of them' (Carter, 1998: 117). Our argument would be that, by providing them with support in the form of existing examples as models, opportunities for discussion and time to gather words relating to the child's existing experiences, we are empowering children who might otherwise lack the confidence to express themselves through poetry.

As well as making frequent use of poetic forms, it is also useful to use specific poems which have a clear structure and which provide models which could be emulated. One such poem used was 'The Secret Box' (by 'Ralph', in Corbett, 1997). Here is one child's response to that poem:

My Secret Box

I found my box.

Locked in an enchanted land

Its sides are made of

Smooth pearl and marble

Its lid is carved by a

lion's roar trapped in a desert

The hinges are made

Of polished silver from

The darkest night.

If you press your ear to

The box you will hear

The sparkle of the stars.

My box contains the

Secret of floating music.

The reader must judge, but for us, the images used by the child are memorable and very much her own. We would argue that the form *enabled* rather than *constrained* her. The idea that a star's sparkle is a sound and that music floats have come into being because the poem used as a model encouraged her to imagine *beyond* her experience.

Here are some other examples of writing inspired by the same poem:

Its sides are made of tough, leathery skin

From a swamp snake from planet Dagobah

and:

> Its sides are made of
>
> Fragile, embroidered peacock feathers

These examples show that different children produced poems individual and unique to them, making connections with aspects of life that interest them (science fiction, nature). Incidentally, all the children in the class experienced a sense of success and a sense of being 'real writers' since these were 'published' as a class anthology, shared with a parallel class and made available for visitors to browse through in the waiting area.

It is worth noting at this point that using particular poems as sources of inspiration is a very inclusive activity. The examples above are taken from a Year 5 class, but, arguably, using poems with strong structures is even more useful for younger children whose experience of both poetry and the world is more restricted. They are very quick to identify particular features of poems and will delight in writing their own poetry inspired by their favourites. Providing forms of poetry as models might be seen as a very inclusive approach, allowing, as it does, all pupils some measure of success. While we would not wish to see models of poetry used strictly as writing frames, they can act as springboards for the more able, while enabling less confident writers to focus on fewer aspects of the writing process and thus be successful. For pupils with English as an additional language, poems which follow a very clear structure can provide a certain amount of support. The opportunities to use 'real', high-quality poems, to engage in word play, to see how writers subvert both word and form, can, Carter (1997) would argue, benefit EAL learners, as:

> to use only those types of dialogue that are transparent and transactional and devoid of richness, cultural reference and creativity is to misrepresent what speakers actually do and simultaneously to lose an opportunity for interesting language awareness work of a kind which may be an ideal precursor to enhanced literary awareness. (Carter, 1997, in Grainger, 2004: 170)

Adding another dimension to this, EAL learners can be encouraged to bring in poems from their own countries and cultures, and use these as scaffolds for writing poetry in both English and their own languages.

Another popular poem which we used in our classrooms as a model for children was 'The Magic Box' by Kit Wright. When this poem was used, a PowerPoint presentation was put together with images which were our own personal response to this poem. While reading the poem to the class, the presentation was played, adding an extra dimension to this shared reading activity. We then presented the children with our very own 'magic box' – a decorated box which contained some of our personal treasures – photographs, jewellery, letters – and the children were invited to explore the contents. Group discussion was then promoted, whereby the children discussed what they might put into their magic box and what it might be made from. All these activities were spread over a week's worth of lessons, immersing children within the ideas inspired by the original poem. Eventually, the children wrote their own poems and below is an example from a pupil in Year 6:

My Magic Box

I will put in the box

A thread from a magic carpet

The colours of a rainbow

The healing powers of a phoenix.

I will put in the box

The horns of a devil

The whiteness of a cloud

A bolt of lightning.

I will put in the box

A clap of thunder

A star from space

A flame of a burning fire.

My box is fashioned from Basalisk skin.

I shall go to an imaginary land in my box.

As in the previous examples, this child has drawn on many sources in order to produce this poem. He has used the structure of the original and has then clearly been inspired by the books he has read and the films he has seen. Interestingly, although it cannot be shown here, this pupil chose to type out his poem and the font and border used was clearly deliberately chosen to 'match' the style, tone and subject matter of his poem.

In all of the above examples, part of the children's success came not only from having read, enjoyed and discussed a wide range of poetry, but on having had a clear focus on 'how did the poet do that/achieve that effect/create that response in the reader?' This is teaching a technique for this particular arts process (Harmer, 2000) as is teaching children how to apply watercolour or engage in role-play:

> They need an understanding of form and the discipline of their materials. (Harmer, 2000: 17)

If we as teachers provide that, then children can begin first to imitate and then experiment and ultimately construct their own. However, Wilson (2007: 453) queries, quite rightly, 'whether some literary forms are more straitjacket than scaffold' and therein lies the skill of the creative teacher in choosing both the form and the best time to introduce it to their pupils:

> At their best, and if wisely chosen by teachers, literary forms do enable children to go further than the original writing, allowing them the opportunity to transform their knowledge both of the form in question and their own experience. (Wilson, 2007: 453)

Conclusion

It would seem therefore, to us, that the use of form is a natural extension of Bruner's (1966) theory of scaffolding to support young learners. As with all scaffolding, there needs to be a gradual withdrawal of support as competence and confidence increases.

(Continued)

(Continued)

Ensuring that children are exposed to a wide range of poems, which include specific poetic forms – haikus, kennings, rhyming couplets, free verse – and carefully chosen poems which have strong, identifiable structures, is a fundamental aspect of enabling and empowering children with their poetry writing. Our aim has always been to remove the fear of the blank page and to demystify the process, for both teachers and children, without reducing poetry to the merely formulaic and mundane, and to emphasise the importance of poetry within the curriculum. Valerie Bloom, herself a popular poet, says that poetry 'is such a concentrated use of language, it can focus the mind in a way that not many other forms do. It encourages precision as well as creativity in writing and allows pupils to view a subject in new and unusual ways, thereby expanding the imagination' (cited in Wilson, 1998: 30). These metacognitive demands are not inconsiderable and that disciplined creativity is surely what is needed for those making their way in a sharply competitive globalised economy. Jill Pirrie would go further:

> A poetic education equips children to engage in lateral thinking and make the kind of imaginative leaps as essential to a technological society as to our spiritual health. The scientists and engineers of the new millennium are not well served by a reductive education manned by the army of foot-soldiers whose job is to obey orders, not to think. (Cited in Wilson, 1998: 40)

It is, therefore, essential that we, as educators, give children every chance to use their own life experiences and combine these with the opportunities we can provide in the classroom in the form of introducing them to high-quality literature, providing time for discussion and the freedom and time to write. With exposure to a wide range of poetry, the structure of different forms and the enrichment of their language, children are empowered to make meaning from their own lives and to reflect upon their own and others' experiences.

We feel very strongly that using poetic form as a starting point for children's own writing is only one way of approaching poetry composition and that ultimately one 'sets children free' to write what they want, how they want and when they want. We feel, however, that in order to reach this stage, children need to be given the 'tools' rather than just being thrown in at the deep end where some will swim but many may well sink. Once one appreciates that 'poetry does for dance what language does for walking – it transforms the mundane into the surprising, the new and the enlightening' (Lambirth, 2007: 7), one can begin to get children to weave their own web of words through their poetry writing. Our approach we hope will enable children to be, in Elizabeth Jennings' words, 'locked into language' but 'with a golden key'.

Something to read

Harrison, M. and Stuart-Clark, C. (eds) *The Oxford Treasury of Classic Poems.* Oxford: Oxford University Press.

Lambirth, A. (2007) *Poetry Matters.* Leicester: UKLA. This slim volume holds a wealth of practical ideas regarding the planning of a poetry unit along with inspiring ideas about how to teach it and to get children writing their own. The focus is clearly on empowering children to use their own lives and experiences as starting points and stresses the benefits of teaching poetry throughout.

Mitton, T. (2010) *Plum*, 2nd edn. London: Barn Owl Books.

Something to think about

Browse through some poetry books. Have a think about which poems would make useful models for children's writing. Often these are poems which have a very clear structure or a regular rhythm, repetition or language patterns. Consider how you might use these poems to support children's initial approaches to poetry writing, but then think about how you could move them on towards more independent writing.

Something to try

Find a favourite poem of your own which has a strong, recognisable structure. Read it several times to absorb the cadence, style and language. Read it aloud, exploring the feel and taste of the ideas as they pass your lips. Consider how you might use the structure of the poem as a vehicle for your own ideas.

References

Brownjohn, S. (1994) *To Rhyme or Not to Rhyme?* London: Hodder & Stoughton.

Bruner, J. (1966) *Toward a Theory of Instruction.* Cambridge, MA: Harvard University Press.

Carter, D. (1998) *Teaching Poetry in the Primary School.* London: David Fulton.

Corbett, P. (1997) *Writing KS1–2 Photocopiable Resource Bank,* Stanley Thornes Blueprints Series. Cheltenham: Stanley Thornes.

Grainger, T. (ed.) (2004) *The RoutledgeFalmer Reader in Literacy.* London: RoutledgeFalmer.

Harmer, D. (2000) 'Poetry in the primary school', *Education 3–13,* 28 (2): 15–18.

Hughes, T. (1963) *Here Today.* London: Hutchinson.

Kress, G. (1994) *Learning to Write,* 2nd edn. London: Routledge.

Kress, G. (2000) '"You made it like a crocodile": a theory of children's meaning making', in T. Grainger (ed.), *The RoutledgeFalmer Reader in Literacy.* London: RoutledgeFalmer.

Lambirth, A. (2007) *Poetry Matters.* Leicester: UKLA.

Meek, M. (1991) *On Being Literate.* London: Bodley Head.

Pirrie, J. (1987) *On Common Ground: A Programme for Teaching Poetry.* Sevenoaks: Hodder & Stoughton Educational.

Pirrie, J. (1994) *On Common Ground: A Programme for Teaching Poetry.* Godalming: World Wildlife Fund.

Rosen, M. (1998) *Did I Hear You Write?,* 2nd edn. Nottingham: Five Leaves Publications.

Sedgwick, F. (1997) *Read My Mind: Young Children's Poetry and Learning.* London: Routledge.

Sedgwick, F. (2000) *Writing to Learn: Poetry and Literacy across the Primary Curriculum.* London: RoutledgeFalmer.

Wilson, A. (2001) 'Brownjohn, Hughes, Pirrie and Rosen: what rhymes with oral writing?', *English in Education*, 35 (2): 3–11.

Wilson, A. (2005) '"Signs of progress": reconceptualising response to children's poetry writing', *Changing English*, 12 (2): 227–42.

Wilson, A. (2007) 'Finding a voice? Do literary forms work creatively in teaching poetry writing?', *Cambridge Journal of Education*, 37: 441–57.

Wilson, A. and Hughes, S. (1998) *The Poetry Book for Primary Schools*. London: Poetry Society.

Wilson, T. (1998) '*The Balloon Man: poetry and the literacy hour*', in A. Wilson and S. Hughes, *The Poetry Book for Primary Schools*. London: Poetry Society.

6

Poetry is slamming: different ways to perform poetry in primary schools

Andrew Lambirth

Chapter Overview

This chapter is all about performing poetry in primary classrooms. I argue that performing poetry should be an integral part of a school day because it is enjoyable and rich in opportunities to learn about poetry and the world. I make the case for how performing poetry that combines movement, language and talk is a mode of learning that has a firm theoretical foundation. I also contend in this chapter that the performance of poetry does not always require an audience and I go on to create a broad typology for performing poetry. Within these three broad categories activities are suggested which I believe will thrill children and encourage them to love poetry forever.

Introduction

Try chanting this: *Bam Ba Litty Bam Bam, Bam Ba Litty Bam Bam, Bam Ba Litty Bam Bam …*

I was introduced to this West Indian saying by Linda Pagett and John Somers (2004). It roughly means: 'I'm telling on you'. I love saying it slowly and then building up speed until I feel I have the tempo just right, savouring its resonances and its multiple applications. It is a wonderful and exhilarating feeling to wrap one's tongue round the words, sounds and rhythms of this simple, short saying. As I am chanting it I begin to move my whole body as a rhythm begins to take hold. I want to start clapping and tapping too. I then begin to be aware that my lips and tongue are generating a rhythm and sound together independent of the noise that is coming from my throat – turn down the volume to a whisper and you can experience what I mean. Now try saying it in different ways. Say it with joy, anger, humour or fear. Try it in different accents – posh, cockney, West Indian, Irish, French, Italian. Can you say it as a question and then as a statement? Whole new meanings can be produced by varying the intonation. Children will enjoy playing with this saying and begin to realise that poetry and word-play in schools is a form of fun that they will recognise and want to embrace. It is then they begin to per-ceive how the artistic affordances of this medium can be utilised for more deep and profound applications.

As the poet Robert Frost rightly stated (as cited in Styles, 1986), 'poetry begins with delight and ends in wisdom'. Much of this delight comes from playing with the sounds and rhythms that words make and the wisdom will come from exploring the meanings that live in this unique mode of artistic representation and commu-nication. Poetry is a glorious fusion of music, speech and movement and poets have realised this for centuries. It is multi-modal (Grainger et al., 2005), naturally demanding the involvement of all these ways of communicating meaning. Performing poetry is a way for everyone involved – speakers and listeners – to respond to the meanings that are invoked. In this chapter I wish to argue for more performance of poetry in classrooms by children, teachers and parents. I want to declare that performing poetry of all kinds will bring joy, wisdom and fraternity, and that classrooms are perfect places for oral and written poetry communities to develop and flourish.

Slamming it with poetry

Performing poetry has been popular for centuries. Some modern manifestations can be found in 'poetry slams' that are held around the world and are becoming increasingly common in the United Kingdom. Savouring the delights of poetry is becoming irresistibly easier to do. Poetry slams were begun by the poet Mark Smith in Chicago, and are competitions between poets. Smith (2010) argues that 'The slam is about poets performing professionally to an audience they care about, allowing that audience to enjoy themselves, while presenting them with the most profound and heartfelt poetry the poets can muster.' Audiences are encouraged to judge the quality of the poetry and the performance and declare a winner at the end. More information can be found on the poetry slam UK website http://www. poetryslam.org.uk/slam.html.

Slams are materialising in most large towns and cities and are often organised in arts festivals. The basic rules of slam poetry are that a poet performs a poem and then three judges, picked at random from the crowd, hold up score cards, as in an Olympic gymnastics competition: 7.8, 8.1, 8.0. The poets compete in heats and then the winners go on to a final. The poems must be original and performed without props, costumes or musical accompaniment. The usual time limit is 3 minutes.

Poetry slams in primary schools hold much potential for encouraging either the composition of poems and their performance or simply the performance of poetry by other poets. Teachers can decide about the need for a competitive element, but a performance poetry event is an exciting and dynamic show for everyone. Children can perform the poems in groups rather than on their own. This form of activity encourages talk, negotiation and, most importantly, response to the poems themselves. As I will discuss later, slams are one manifestation of performance and some forms of performing poems require no audience at all.

Performance as response

To enable children to respond to poems through performance, they need to be exposed to and be able to choose from a great many high-quality poems. For this reason it is crucial that we know and delight in poetry ourselves. Fortunately, I can say with complete confidence that we all enjoy poetry and rhyme already. If we do not read it in books than we listen to it through music – popular or classical – and we are regularly moved by it both physically and emotionally in its various manifestations. Rhymes are always used by the advertising industry to sell products. They are shrewd and wily enough to know what rhyme can do, how we can catch it on our lips and tongue and how it helps us remember names and narratives. Since childhood we will have found pleasures in rhyme – laying in our parents' arms or at bath time – and would have sung and chanted it as we tumbled out of the school gates. So I know we all enjoy it. But we need to do more. Here are a few ideas to start you off:

- buy one good anthology of poems written for adults that provides a tour of poetry through history;

- find a time to read one poem every day;

- talk about them with loved ones, friends or colleagues;

- have at least six good children's poetry books in the classroom library;

- read them yourself and to the children and decide the ones you like and observe the ones the children like too.

As teachers we need to know why we do the things we do with the children in schools. What is it that performance poetry activities are doing for the children intellectually? What are they learning? Is it just fun? To find out we can turn to Vygotsky (1978) and Bruner (1983). They both took the view that knowledge is always the product of human enquiry and invention rather than something given to us by nature. They believed that the knowledge we possess comes from our social interaction with others in our culture and it is this process that gives meaning to our experiences of the world. However, knowledge cannot simply be communicated or transmitted from one to another; it must be reconstructed by the learner. This makes talk essential to how we learn, by its ability to enable us to re-represent new knowledge for ourselves. Olson states that discovery of knowledge 'is possible only by constructing understandings on the basis of extensions, elaborations or reformulations of current preceding understandings' (2001: 105). Vygotsky argues that 'speech turns inwards and becomes inner speech or internal language, both interacting with and influencing the thinking and the learning process' (Cordon, 2000: 8). For Vygotsky (1978: 57) 'every function in the child's cultural development appears twice: first on the social level and later on the individual level' as cultural activities are internalised by the learner.

These theories suggest that cultural activities, particularly those that involve talk and other physical actions, are internalised and take on an intellectual manifestation which forms the basis of knowledge. It could be said then, as a result of this position, that performing poetry creates the possibilities of learning how to *think* about poetry – through talk and interaction. Performing it enables children to feel the rhythms that come from its structures and forms. In the process of performance they will need to draw on their own experiences of movement and their own established meanings about the world to interpret and respond to poetry through performance. All this is internalised; it moves from the social, active and dynamic to the personal and the intellectual. Children will *know* how to read and make meaning from poetry because they have lived it with others in the culture. In the same way that we learn to make calculations in our heads by having first experienced physically jumping along number squares placed on the floor by teachers, used our fingers, toes or plastic blocks to count and discussed the processes involved, so too responding to poetry through performance enables us to read and understand poetry ourselves as a personal and intellectual act because our whole body has been involved. We internalise these experiences which become part of our thoughts. If we agree with this theoretical perspective then it would appear that performing poetry is a powerful way of learning to read and understand it. The physical act of performing poetry alongside the verbal negotiations children have with teachers and other children about the meanings of poetry and its affect is a social act of interaction which helps form the basis of their new knowledge about poetry.

Ong (1982) informs us how bodily activity forms part of oral communication, and certainly poets use physical movement in the composition of their poems. Heaney (1980) discusses the significance of Wordsworth's walking to and fro on his gravel path: 'the swing of the poet's body contributed to the sway of his voice' and this is found in some of the rhythms in Wordsworth's poetry. Caribbean poet Valerie Bloom explains how performing poetry was central to her introduction to this form of writing:

> Poetry was never read, it was always performed. We used to have tea parties at school where the school would put on sessions to raise funds for the school. There would be people performing and some food, like curry goat and rice and peas. (Hoyles and Hoyles, 2003: 29)

Benjamin Zephaniah has also explained the importance of movement and performance in his work:

> Most of my poems start in my head with the rhythm ... and I'll pace up and down the room as I'm saying it, and sometimes I'm actually kind of dancing ... For me, one of the most important things about poems is how they're said. When they roll off the tongue nicely, that's when I know that they're ready for writing down. (Zephaniah, 2001: 18)

Poems demand to be heard, they demand to be performed and asking children to do this is as powerful a process as their very composition. The way children choose to respond and perform poems – their use of voice and intonation, their physical actions – all are indications of the meanings the children are taking from the poems themselves.

Performing poetry

So far I have tried to establish why performing poetry is worthwhile and exciting. I now want to suggest what teachers can do to encourage children to lift poetry off the page and into the classroom space and beyond. Here I wish to make a distinction between the different manifestations of 'performance'. To me, performance poetry does not always need an audience. This may seem strange, but sometimes the performance can be simply the response itself, made by the individual or group. Performing for an audience can require radically different skills than performances that are a reflection of how a group of children have responded to a poem. So children working with PPD (poetry process drama – see below) may never need to perform for anyone but themselves. Drama and drama techniques are used as a device for getting to know the poem and the meanings the children feel it invokes.

So, I would like to suggest categorising performance poetry as follows:

- *Slamming*. Learning and recitation singularly or in groups – here much of the emphasis is on the performance of the poems themselves – performance of the words takes centre stage. In slamming there is a product, which is the performance. The process of getting to the performance is crucial and rich in learning, but the emphasis is on the quality of the performance itself.

- *Poetry process drama (PPD).* Includes the use of drama techniques like freeze frames and conscience tunnels/corridors. Emphasis here is on the process of working in groups with a poem and its representation in the form of dramatic scenarios or techniques that encourage responses. For this form of work the learning is centred on process, and the performance side is directed to the individuals involved rather than any audience. Children can take on roles of the characters in poems; they may extend interactions between characters in a poem, inventing new conversations and scenarios that happen beyond what the text provides. Here, the children are required to consider events and characters in depth, sculpting their ideas into new situations with the material initially provided by the poem itself.

- *Singing and chanting.* This kind of poetry performance can be for an audience or just a class of children singing and chanting simply for the love of it. The emphasis here is on the music, rhythm and rhyme and the creativity needed to make a poem come alive by a group of children working together to sing and chant the meanings off the page.

I shall now explore these three categories in more depth.

Slamming

I believe strongly that performing poetry for an audience, as in the case of slamming, is best done when the children have memorised the poem. This can be done collectively as a group, with the individual children learning sections of the poem, or singularly – the lone child reciting the whole poem. For this to be done well, children must be shown the joys of memorising poems. Ted Hughes provides good advice here:

> There are many reasons for learning poems. But memorising them should be a game. It should be a pleasure. For those of us who need help (nearly all of us), the method most commonly used in schools is learning by rote. This is one of several memorising techniques. And for most people it is the least effective … the cost can be heavy, since it creates an aversion to learning and to poetry. (Hughes, 1997: ix)

These are words we all need to remember when we ask children to learn poetry for a slam or some other performance. Hughes goes on to suggest the brain can memorise and recall better by connecting the words and lines with a visual image – the more absurd or exaggerated the image the better. Children may want to produce a reproduction of their poem that they need to learn. Illustrations can be made for each line or for words that are particularly tricky to recall. However one tries to remember a poem, the process must be devoid of any fear. The whole exercise is about pleasure, and without this pleasure there will be no learning. When children learn a poem they may keep it with them for the rest of their lives. They can bring the poem out whenever they feel the need, it will always be there, like an old friend to comfort or amuse. As I have said earlier, choosing poems for children to learn can be an act of negotiation between the teacher and the children, but a knowledge of great poets and poems will always power the activity and the result. Alternatively, children may wish to recite either their own poems or the songs and rhymes they may know already. Slams with these rhymes can also be very rewarding and entertaining.

Here are some ideas to get children slamming:

- Reintroduce skipping ropes into the playground. In the classroom collect all the rhymes for skipping the children know (see Chapter 4 for more ideas).

- Boys too like to skip with the girls (I did when I was a child!), but if they do not, ask the boys to recite football chants and pop songs they know. There will be a rich collection of subverted and sometimes 'naughty' songs and rhymes.

- Hold a class assembly that celebrates the lore of the playground. The passing of poems to others by word of mouth has a rich historical tradition that lives on with children in the playground. Bring in a rope to the performance space and enjoy them together as a whole school or Key Stage.

- Make a class book that 'freezes' the rhymes common at the time of production.

- Bring in a collection of poems that you know the children will like to perform. Let them choose the ones they like. Read them aloud to the children, perhaps with the help of your teaching assistant, bringing them to life and modelling the fun of reciting poetry. Ask the children in groups of four or five to learn and perform their chosen poem.

- You may wish to organise a slam between classes in a Key Stage for the parents one afternoon. You may also have a more modest aim of asking the children to go around the classes in the school performing poems. This could be done as a 'surprise poetry attack' to the class in the middle of a lesson. Let poetry make an impact – guerrilla poetry performances!

- Videoing performances for presentation on the web via an intranet system is also fun. The children could e-mail their performances to their friends in other schools or their parents at home, sending the performance as an attachment.

Poetry process drama (PPD)

Process drama is widely used in primary schools to engage children in the fictional worlds that can be found in texts of all kinds. It has been seen to assist children's learning of literacy in many ways (for example, Barrs and Cork, 2001). It works well with poetry too. One needs to remember that it is all about the process and there is no need to perform their work to an audience. The experience of imaginatively entering the world of the poem is where the learning is found. Below are a number of drama techniques which can be used with children reading poetry:

- *Meetings.* A useful starting point for drama which allows the giving of information and planning of action with everyone, including the teacher, in role. The teacher meets the children in role as a person from the poem or someone associated with characters and events in the poem. It may be the start of a longer dramatic scenario.

- *Teacher-in-role.* The teacher works alongside pupils in role as a character in a poem. This helps to provide contexts for drama. In Kit Wright's (2009) 'Me', for example, the teacher may introduce herself as the mum in the poem who is on the diet. She may wish to describe 'her lot' and ask the children in the class to follow her down to meet one of her sons who is mending the motorbike, perhaps played by another of the children. In order to bring the children into this imaginary world, the teacher may ask the children to draw an invisible mirror with their finger and then ask them to wink and step through. The teacher in role might then ask for suggestions on how she can secretly break the diet without the rest of the family knowing and ask them to help her prepare a decent meal. Suddenly the poem, its events and characters are blown off the page into the classroom and into the minds of the children. By becoming one of the characters and engaging in the conversations they may have, the children begin to understand the family relationships and people and their problems. Drama scenarios like this one can last for up to an hour in some cases. At the end the children will need to step back through the mirror to return them to their 'primary world' of the classroom. 'Me' is a short simple poem, so working with longer narrative poems holds so much potential.

- *Freeze frame.* Freeze frames can represent feelings, characters, events and atmosphere by means of a human tableau. The children form a shape using their bodies that represents a particular aspect of the poem. So, they may wish to represent the meaning of particular stanzas or the whole of the poem, the feelings of the characters, the atmosphere the poem invokes and so on. Teachers often keep the title of the poem secret before reading and then ask the children to make a freeze frame that they think may represent the title. Once again, we must model freeze frames with the children.

- *Hot-seating.* Groups as themselves question the teacher in role or child in role to find out about character and situation.

- *Role on the wall.* An outline drawing of a character from the poem is placed on the wall or board. Pupils write their thoughts and feelings about characters on pieces of paper and attach them round the drawing. Inside the body outline might be how the children perceive the character to think about herself and outside the body may be what others think about her.

- *Thought-tracking.* Individuals in role are asked to speak aloud their private thoughts and feelings relating to events.

- *Conscience tunnel.* Two lines of children face each other, forming a tunnel. One child walks down the tunnel receiving advice from the others who attempt to ignite the character's conscience regarding a particular situation/event from a poem.

Grainger and Cremin (2001) argue that process drama is rich in its power to show children the appeal of entering fictional worlds. They also provide super examples of how to work with texts.

Singing and chanting

Poetry has long been associated with music and song and we love chanting and clapping and making our own music in our own way. Playground rhyme is full of chanting and clapping and slapping. Just think of the rhymes for picking teams like 'One Potato, Two Potato, Three Potato, Four'. This invites children to chant in different ways. One child may wish to chant the first word of each line while the others chant all the potatoes. Instruments can be introduced, words can be omitted and replaced with these un-pitched instruments – all sorts of fun can be gleaned from this one rhyme.

Once again, teachers may choose to use published poems and rhymes to chant or may ask children to devise their own. I love the idea Michael Rosen introduced to me and a group of teachers in London many years ago. He suggested that we ask the children to remember three things that their parents say that drive them mad and write them down. For example, my father used to say to me 'leave things alone' whenever I had touched something which had spilt or snapped or fallen over. Children will remember all sorts of quotes: 'were you born in a barn?'; 'be in by six'; 'when I was young ...' and so on. The children, in negotiation with their friends, decide on the best one and they choose it to say out loud. The teacher begins with their quote and then goes round the class hearing each one, eventually returning to the teacher who says theirs again. A performance. I have done this with many classes and I like to enhance it by selecting children to come out to the front of the class. The children chant their quote again, but this time, after every three quotes the class add a chorus of 'That's what my mum says, that's what my mum says'. It is always very funny.

Reciting poems together, using instruments and the use of different groupings of voices for different parts of the poem always works well and makes a great performance, but it is also just wonderful for children to work together for their own pleasure. Multiple voices can work in a round, for example. Take a simple rhyme from Anon.: 'There she goes, there she goes, all dressed up in her Sunday clothes'. This works well as a round for three people. Each person takes a line and says it three times. One person starts their line after the previous person and so on. Poetry loves to be used in this way as this is what much of it was made for.

Conclusion

In this chapter I have argued for more performance of poetry in schools. I have suggested that by performing poetry children will gain knowledge about how to read and enjoy it. I have differentiated between different ways of performing poetry: slamming, poetry process drama work (PPD), and singing and chanting. I have argued that performing poetry needs no audience other than the participants themselves, but that some performances like poetry slams cannot live without them. Each way of performing poetry needs different skills, but all will enhance children's love of poetry. I predict that once you start performing poetry with your class, you will not want to stop, and what is more, you know it is doing them good!

Something to read

Barrs, M. and Rosen, M. (1997) *A Year with Poetry*. London: Centre for Literacy in Primary Education. A superb record of teachers working with poetry in primary schools in London.

Something to think about

What is poetry? Have you ever considered what makes a poem a poem? What are its special features? What can it do for a reader and a writer that prose cannot? I think it is an important question for teachers to consider as a team and to discuss. You may wish to read around what writers and poets say about the essence of poetry.

Something to try

By reading poetry anthologies, establish your six favourite children's poets. Look for poets who are less familiar to you, but whose work you really admire. Share your choices with the children and find out if they like them too.

References

Barrs, M. and Cork, V. (2001) *The Reader in the Writer: The Influence of Literature Upon Writing at KS2*. London: Centre for Literacy in Primary Education.

Barrs, M. and Rosen, M. (1997) *A Year with Poetry*. London: Centre for Literacy in Primary Education.

Bruner, J. (1983) *Child's Talk: Learning to Use Language*. Oxford: Oxford University Press.

Cordon, R. (2000) *Literacy and Learning Through Talk: Strategies for the Primary Classroom*. Buckingham: Open University Press.

Grainger, T. and Cremin, M. (2001) *Resourcing Drama in the Classroom 8–14*. Sheffield: National Association for the Teaching of English.

Grainger, T., Goouch, K. and Lambirth, A. (2005) *Creativity and Writing: Developing Voice and Verve in the Classroom*. Abingdon: Routledge.

Heaney, S. (1980) *Preoccupations*. London: Faber & Faber.

Hoyles, A. and Hoyles, B. (2003) 'Black performance poetry', *English in Education*, 37 (1): 27–38.

Hughes, T. (ed.) (1997) *By Heart: 101 Poems to Remember*. London: Faber & Faber.

Olson, D. (2001) 'Education: the bridge from culture to mind', in D. Bakhurst and S. G. Shanker (eds), *Jerome Bruner: Language, Culture and Self*. London: Sage.

Ong, W. J. (1982) *Orality and Literacy: The Technologising of the Word*. London: Methuen.

Pagett, L. and Somers, J. (2004) *Off by Heart: Performing and Presenting Poetry in the Primary School*. Sheffield: National Association for the Teaching of English.

Smith, M. (2010) Online at: http://www.poetryslam.org.uk/slam.html (accessed August 2010).

Styles, M. (1986) *Start Writing: Helping Children to Begin Writing Poetry*. London: EARO.

Vygotsky, L. (1978) *Thought and Language*. Cambridge: MA: MIT Press.

Wright, K. (2009) *The Magic Box: Poems for Children*. London: Macmillan.

Zephaniah, B. (2001) 'Poetry', in J. Carver (ed.), *Creating Writers: A Creative Writing Manual for Schools*. London: Routledge.

Section 3

Non-fiction

7

Inspiring and enthusing children as readers and writers of non-fiction

Michael Green

Chapter Overview

This chapter will explore how creative teachers support children in becoming successful and enthusiastic readers and writers of non-fiction. It will focus on the importance of choosing the right text and the need to embed children's experiences of reading and writing non-fiction in meaningful contexts which relate to their interests and experiences both in and outside of school. It will consider what children need to learn about non-fiction, the different types of non-fiction texts along with examples of how to teach them. Suggestions will be made relating to how a cross-curricular approach can be adopted for the teaching of non-fiction. In addition, the role of ICT will be considered. Throughout the chapter I will also focus on the teacher's role in the teaching of non-fiction at a practical level and the process of teaching children about non-fiction within literacy.

Introduction

Non-fiction is ever-present in our lives as adults: filling in forms, browsing the Internet, using social networking sites, reading the newspaper, writing lists, writing reminder notes, texting on our mobile phones, e-mailing friends and family, watching documentaries on TV ... the list is endless. The same can also be said of the children we will teach. Out of the classroom, the vast majority of texts on paper and on screen that children encounter are non-fiction. For many years though, the diet of text types children encountered within the primary classroom centred mainly around narrative and poetic genres (Wray and Lewis, 1997). Rarely did children encounter explicit teaching of reading and writing non-fiction. One key underlying issue identified centred around teachers having a limited knowledge and understanding of non-fiction texts. The introduction of the National Literacy Strategy in 1998 (DfEE, 1998) certainly made a positive step towards addressing the imbalance of children's literary text experiences. However, as Lewis (2009) argues, while the introduction of the NLS framework had a positive impact on widening teachers' knowledge of non-fiction texts, much of children's experiences were decontextualised, skill-based lessons rather than experiences set in meaningful and purposeful contexts. Such activities are certainly not beneficial to children if they are being carried out in isolation without any real purpose or application in other work. How then does the creative literacy teacher use non-fiction in purposeful contexts which engage and interest children? What follows is an exploration of what I consider to be key principles in the effective teaching of non-fiction in the primary classroom.

What is non-fiction?

Before we go on to explore these principles, we must first consider what we mean by non-fiction. Definitions are very wide ranging and, as Lewis (2009) points out, with constant advances in technology, new ways of creating and accessing non-fiction texts continue to emerge and the term 'non-fiction' continues to expand. This puts teachers in an exciting, yet daunting position.

For many years now non-fiction in primary education has been, for the most part, focused around six genres:

- recount texts;

- explanatory texts;

- instructional texts;

- persuasive texts;

- non-chronological reports;

- discursive texts.

These six genres have been termed the 'language of power' (Wray and Lewis, 2004). Drawing on the work by linguists Martin and Rothery (1980, 1981, 1986) who originally grouped non-fiction into these six categories, Wray and Lewis (2004: 417) argue that children who leave our classrooms 'unable to operate successfully within these powerful genres are denied access to becoming fully functioning members of society'. As Martin (1989) points out, adult daily interaction with text centres around non-fiction so it stands to reason that we need to equip children to meet the demands of the world in which they live. Being confident readers and writers of non-fiction ensures that we are able to access information and articulate our knowledge and understanding of the world. Take a moment to reflect on your interaction with text today – how much of it is non-fiction?

Creative teachers of literacy need to have an awareness of the linguistic and organisational features of these six genres. How do we know a piece of writing is persuasive? What are the language features of instructional writing? It is essential that teachers have this awareness and are confident in selecting authentic and engaging materials to use in the classroom to motivate and inspire primary children. Towards the end of this chapter I will explore this further. However, it is also important to point out that not all forms of writing conform strictly to the characteristic features of these genres. This is one of the main criticisms levelled against documents such as *Grammar for Writing* (DfEE, 2000) which identified the characteristic features of the six genres; but following this to the letter could result in 'an inflexible view of the range of text types "permitted"' (Lewis 2009: 129). The very fact that many examples that you will encounter do not strictly conform is, for me, the exciting part of demonstrating to children how you can cross boundaries in writing and play with language to suit the purpose and the audience. Teachers need to be able to confidently exploit the rich and varied material available to them, including ICT, and recognise that texts do not fit neatly into the six categories previously mentioned.

I shall now explore some ways in which to inspire and enthuse children to be confident readers and writers of non-fiction.

Using children's existing experiences and interests

The skilful teacher acknowledges that children enter their classroom with a rich understanding and experience of the world around them (Barnes, 2007). This is of particular importance when considering how to engage and motivate children to read and write non-fiction. Children's personal interests need to be recognised and these interests exploited to provide an authentic and meaningful context for children's writing of non-fiction. As teachers, we have the tendency to select the subject matter that the children in our classes are going to write about. Should this be the case? Does it really matter what the subject matter is? Why shouldn't we empower the children to select the subject matter? What follows is one example of how a teacher did just this.

The children in a Year 3 class were due to start their new literacy unit focusing on information texts and their teacher wished to create an authentic situation. She identified a shortage of information books in the school library and used this opportunity for the children to write their own information books on subjects that interested them so that they could be added to the school collection of books. This type of contextualised, purposeful activity was key to motivating the children to write their own information books on a subject matter that interested and engaged them and that they could write about with passion and enthusiasm. It also provided the children with a real audience for their writing.

Prior to starting their unit of work the children were set the task of collecting real-life examples of information texts on topics that interested them. The vast range of topics that children chose was amazing! Topics ranged from the art of decoupage to football annuals. This wealth of material provided the teacher with the ideal starting point for getting the children to begin to explore the features of the texts, drawing out similarities and differences and discussing how the purpose and audience of each text may have influenced the layout.

Before children can begin to write, it is essential that they are immersed in the kind of texts that they are going to write and that they actively explore the texts, reading and understanding the information. The children in this example engaged in research on their chosen subjects, drawing on texts, ICT-based material and their own knowledge and understanding. The children gave 'expert' talks on their chosen subjects as a means of orally rehearsing the content. The children used skeleton frames (Palmer, 2001) as a means of note-taking. Through teacher modelling and shared composition, the children were then ready to begin to shape their own information books.

From the example above it can be seen that using children's own experiences and interests as a starting point had a number of important benefits:

- The children were extremely motivated as they were focusing on areas that interested them and which they had chosen.

- The children were put in the powerful position of 'expert', writing about a topic that they were familiar with and interested in. This gave the children the confidence to write.

- It provided the teacher with the ideal opportunity to get to know the interests and out-of-school pursuits of the children in her class.

For the interested reader, Sue Palmer's book entitled *How to Teach Writing Across the Curriculum* (2001) provides a number of useful examples of how to use skeleton frames to support children's writing of non-fiction texts.

The children in the example above made good use of ICT during their projects. The next section will consider the role of ICT and how teachers can exploit the potential of new technologies to inspire children as readers and writers of non-fiction.

Harnessing the potential of new technologies

Children today have been born into a technological revolution and instinctively look to technology within their everyday lives (Hague and Williamson, 2009). A recent survey of 3,001 pupils aged between 8 and 16 in England and Scotland by the National Literacy Trust (2009) found that 82 per cent of those children surveyed wrote text messages at least once a month, 73 per cent used instant messaging as a means of communicating and 63 per cent used social networking sites such as Bebo. Indeed, as Davies and Merchant (2009) argue, digital practices such as social networking are now so embedded in society that they should be part of the literacy curriculum. More often, however, children's interactivity with technology has to be left at the school gate and they enter a school environment in which technology has an entirely different face. How then can we exploit the potential of ICT to ensure that our classrooms are full of enthusiastic readers and writers of non-fiction? Below are just a few examples.

Using podcasts

An increasing number of schools are making use of podcasts to share children's work with a wider audience via the Internet. One of the main benefits for using podcasts is that it provides pupils with a potential global audience for their work and this supplies many children with the necessary motivation (Willet, 2009). In addition, as mentioned previously, providing the children with a real purpose to their work is crucial if we are to engage them. There is a considerable range of activities involving the use of podcasts which lend themselves nicely to non-fiction. By far the most common is in the form of a radio broadcast by the children reporting on current topics and activities. Some schools are now using this as an alternative to the newsletter. The process of writing and recording a podcast provides the children with an authentic opportunity for them to develop their non-fiction writing skills, alongside their ICT skills. It also provides an excellent opportunity for children to work collaboratively in a group situation. Interestingly, research by Becta (2010) identified the top two favoured ways of learning by children as learning in groups and doing something practical. Free software packages are available online to get you started with podcasting. One that is used by many is called Audacity.

Blogging

The purpose of many blogs is to provide information and opinion on a particular subject that interests the author. As Scott (2001) notes, blogs primarily take the form of a diary, journal, 'what's new' page or links to other websites. Typically they are multi-modal, combining text, images, sounds and video related to the subject. The ability of readers to leave comments in an interactive format is an important feature of many blogs. According to recent research by the National Literacy Trust (2009), pupils who regularly blog perceive themselves to be 'good' at writing.

According to the research, 24 per cent of those surveyed had their own personal blogs and regularly updated them. Again, one key benefit of blogging is that it provides pupils with a virtual 'stage' on which to perform their writing skills to a far-reaching audience. The availability of free blogging software such as PrimaryBlogger makes blogging a perfect means of applying children's non-fiction writing skills in a purposeful and meaningful way. It is worth looking online at examples of primary school blogs. Sandaig Primary School in Glasgow, for example, has been using blogs with its children since 2004.

These are just two ideas for incorporating new technology into your literacy lessons. Obviously these are not the only ways of engaging and inspiring children through the use of ICT. New technologies are forever developing. It is important that teachers keep abreast of these developments so as to reduce the gap between children's home and school experiences.

Using drama to motivate readers and writers of non-fiction

Children learn best through active, physical approaches to learning (Barnes, 2007). As Gardner (1993) points out, 'passive experiences' tend to have minimal lasting impact on learning. Drama provides the perfect vehicle through which the creative teacher of literacy can support children to actively explore non-fiction texts, as well as providing an ideal opportunity for children to orally rehearse the genre before committing pen to paper. In the past, the use of drama within the primary classroom has tended to occur with narrative rather than non-fiction. The innovative teacher will seek opportunities to use drama opportunities within their non-fiction genre study. However, as Cremin (2009) notes, it is essential to create 'thoughtful bridges' between the drama conventions and the writing.

Below I will briefly explore several drama techniques and how they can link to non-fiction:

- *Decision alley and discursive writing*. Excellent ways of representing arguments for and against a subject or decision. The children could take on the roles of particular people such as experts and campaigners.

- *Freeze-frame and instructional writing*. This combination provides the ideal opportunity for children to sequence a set of instructions. Groups of children can freeze-frame the instructions, digital photographs can be taken and then text can be added to the freeze-frames.

- *Hot-seating and recount writing*. A great way for children to explore an event from someone's perspective. The teacher or a child could take on the role of a historical figure, famous sports personality, etc. and be questioned by the remainder of the class. This is an effective probing technique whereby children can learn about a character's motives, feelings and behaviour.

Other useful techniques include improvisation, teacher in role, forum theatre, mantle of the expert and role-play. Below is an example of how role-play can be used within Key Stage 1 and the Foundation Stage.

The role-play area can provide the ideal opportunity to build on young children's existing experiences of the world around them. The Early Years Foundation Stage recommends play as a language learning opportunity. When considering how the role-play area can support young children's understanding of non-fiction, think about organising the area around real-life situations.

Examples include visits to the hospital, the dentist, the veterinary surgery, travel agents, the bank, the post office, the supermarket, a restaurant. All of these situations provide the creative teacher with an opportunity to engage the children with real, purposeful opportunities to promote speaking and listening, writing and playing with language.

For the interested reader, it is worth reading Teresa Cremin's chapter entitled 'Developing drama creatively' in her book *Teaching English Creatively* (2009).

Non-fiction and cross-curricular activities

The current weekly timetable in primary schools is very 'top heavy' with literacy, numeracy and science, leaving other subjects with limited time. Because of this, we need to use literacy lessons as the vehicle for expanding upon other areas of the curriculum, creating meaningful contexts in which the children can apply their reading, writing, speaking and listening skills. It has been argued that cross-curricular approaches within the primary classroom provide greater motivation for children (Barnes, 2007) and research for the Organisation for Economic Cooperation and Development (OECD, 2003) identifies motivation as the key to learning. Many of the texts that children will encounter while engaging with the curriculum are non-fiction (Wray, 2006). Adopting a cross-curricular approach with the teaching of non-fiction while making meaningful links to other areas of the curriculum, therefore, seems very appropriate. Below is one example of how a teacher combined eye-witness report writing within a historical context.

In a Year 5 class the children were learning about the Anglo-Saxons. The teacher identified several writing opportunities that could arise from the children's history work, one of which included an eyewitness report about the Battle of Hastings. As Palmer (2001) points out, if children have become 'experts' on a particular topic it makes sense to link their writing to cross-curricular learning.

The children studied several different sources about the Battle of Hastings, ranging from the Bayeux Tapestry to information books about the event. The children had been learning about mind-mapping so they used this technique to make notes. Armed with sufficient knowledge the teacher planned a role-play opportunity whereby children re-enacted the Battle of Hastings in the school hall, dressing up as the Normans and Anglo-Saxons. This re-enactment enabled the children to have a 'lived experience' of the event and enabled them to orally rehearse and refine their ideas for their eyewitness writing activity. What follows is one child's eyewitness report after the role-play:

> Today has been a truly devastating day for our country! We thought that because we had won all our vicious and hard battles this one against William the Bastard and his evil beasts the Normans would be easy. How naive we were. We were absolutely exhausted after our journey from York to Hastings we had no time to rest before our big fight.
>
> When we saw William's men from Senlac Hill and when William's men tried to break through our shield wall his men were hacked down and slaughtered where they once stood. But alas, King Harold's two most beloved brothers, Leafwin and Gryth, were both killed brutally by those disgusting Normans. At that moment we thought victory was ours and when the Normans retreated down the hill we thought we had won. Without Harold's instructions we charged down from the hill victoriously after the Normans. But despite everything, the Normans had tricked us! They sent out their cavalry and broke through our defences. Our defence was in pieces! But the Normans

weren't done with us yet. The worst was yet to come ... One of the Norman soldiers fired an arrow up in the air and struck our beloved king in the eye! As he fell to his knees in pain we were helpless. The Normans found new strength and finished us off. We had lost!

What is clear from this child's written work is that it has what Cremin (2009) describes as 'passion and pace' in the writing. This child has a clear understanding of the language and organisational features of a typical eyewitness account but has used the drama activity to inject their writing with a real sense of empathy. In addition, their knowledge and understanding of the events of the Battle of Hastings has been enhanced.

While there are many benefits to using a cross-curricular approach for inspiring and enthusing children as readers and writers of non-fiction, there are also several criticisms which need to be considered:

- One criticism of using the cross-curricular approach in writing non-fiction concerns the issue of pupil subject knowledge. It is essential that prior to writing the children are actively engaged in research and information gathering to ensure that they are armed with sufficient knowledge to write about the subject. If they do not have the subject knowledge it will hamper their ability to write in the genre.

- Another issue concerns the focus of the marking by the teacher – should it be on the accuracy of the content or the writing? I would argue that as this is a literacy lesson the marking should focus primarily on the child's writing skills rather than the accuracy of the content.

For the interested reader it is worth reading Jonathan Barnes' book entitled *Cross-Curricular Learning 3–14* (2007) for a more in-depth discussion regarding cross-curricular learning and teaching.

Above I have focused primarily on practical ways of enthusing and inspiring children to be readers and writers of non-fiction. One important element that also needs to be considered is the selection of texts to use. The next section will consider what we should look for when selecting quality non-fiction texts.

Selecting non-fiction texts

It has already been established that the choice of text is crucial if we are to engage, inspire and enthuse children to read and write non-fiction. What then should we look for when selecting non-fiction texts? In a recent discussion with trainee teachers on what they considered to be the 'quality' indicators, the following criteria were developed:

- The use of authentic texts is key. Select real texts which have a real purpose. According to Clipson-Boyles (1999) this is the essential ingredient of a literate classroom. For example, if looking at the use of persuasive language use real advertisements. Remember as well the importance of multi-modal and ICT-based texts, for example radio and TV advertising, advertising banners and pop-ups on the Internet.

- Select texts that are likely to arouse curiosity and interest the children. The key to this is knowing your children!

- Consider ways of selecting texts which will link to other areas of the curriculum being studied.

- Remember that authentic, quality texts will not always conform rigidly to the six 'pure' genres identified previously in the chapter. Many texts will cross boundaries and provide excellent opportunities to explore with children how the purpose and intended audience has influenced the layout and language used.

- Consider texts which will inspire girls. Think about the girls in your class and their interests. This is of particular importance as research tells us that a large proportion of girls do not, out of choice, select non-fiction reading material for enjoyment (Lockwood, 2008).

- Consider the layout of the text – remember that non-fiction texts do not always read sequentially: the text may not read from left to right and top to bottom. Instead it may be of a more complex format with the use of subheadings, text boxes and illustrations, diagrams or photographs to supplement the main body of the text. Ensure that children experience information that is presented in a variety of ways, again linking this to the purpose and audience and how this impacts on the chosen layout.

Remember that the effective teacher will be confident with the text selected and have already identified from the text the potential teaching opportunities that could arise. Remember though to be flexible to respond to children's interests and needs.

For the interested reader, Margaret Mallet's book entitled *Young Researchers: Informational Reading and Writing in the Early and Primary Years* elaborates on many of the 'quality' indicators identified above.

Conclusion

To summarise then, what does the effective literacy teacher need to do in order to inspire and engage children so that they are able to enjoy and benefit from their study of non-fiction texts? Firstly, it stands to reason that teachers themselves need to have a sound knowledge and understanding of the genres, but also be flexible and creative with their teaching approach. The key to this is using active approaches to explore and respond to the texts – drama and role-play, ICT and making those crucial cross-curricular links. Effective teachers need to be able to plan authentic, meaningful contexts for reading and writing rather than artificial activities, drawing on children's own knowledge and experiences. The selection of texts is also vital to successful teaching. The creative teacher will be confident to draw on a wide and varied range of texts, including electronic texts and will also consider their children's interests and reading preferences. Above all, the successful teacher will, themselves, be an enthusiastic lover of non-fiction!

Something to read

Michael Lockwood's *Promoting Reading for Pleasure in the Primary School* (2008) has some excellent case studies to give you plenty of ideas.

Something to think about

Consider your classroom library – do you have a range of non-fiction texts in your classroom library, including authentic texts? Do you take account of popular culture and include children's magazines, football cards, etc. in your reading area? Do you encourage children to choose non-fiction as their reading material? Do you share non-fiction texts aloud with your class? We often share fiction with children but why should non-fiction be any different?

Something to try

Try incorporating new technologies such as blogs, wikis and podcasts into your literacy curriculum.

References

Barnes, J. (2007) *Cross-Curricular Learning 3–14*. London: Sage.

Becta (2010) *21st Century Teacher*. Coventry: Becta.

Carrington, V. and Robinson, M. (eds) (2009) *Digital Literacies: Social Learning and Classroom Practice*. London: Sage.

Clipson-Boyles, S. (1999) 'The role of drama in the literate classroom', in P. Goodwin (ed.), *The Literate Classroom*. London: David Fulton.

Cremin, T. (ed.) (2009) *Teaching English Creatively*. London: Routledge.

Cremin, T., Burnard, P. and Craft, A. (2006) 'Pedagogy and possibility thinking in the Early Years', *International Journal of Thinking Skills and Creativity*: 1 (2): 108–19.

Davies, J. and Merchant, G. (2009) *Web 2.0 for Schools: Learning and Social Participation*. New York: Peter Lang.

DfEE (1998) *The National Literacy Strategy: Framework for Teaching*. London: HMSO.

DfEE (2000) *Grammar for Writing*. London: HMSO.

Gardner, H. (1993) *Frames of Mind: The Theory of Multiple Intelligences*. New York: Basic Books.

Hague, C. and Williamson, B. (2009) *Digital Participation, Digital Literacy and School Subjects: A Review of the Policies, Literature and Evidence*. Bristol: Futurelab.

Lewis, M. (2009) 'Exploring non-fiction texts creatively', in T. Cremin (ed.), *Teaching English Creatively*. London: Routledge.

Lockwood, M. (2008) *Promoting Reading for Pleasure in the Primary School*. London: Sage.

Mallet, M. (1999) *Young Researchers: Informational Reading and Writing in the Early and Primary Years*. Oxford: Routledge.

Martin, J. (1989) *Factual Writing: Exploring and Challenging Social Reality*. Oxford: Oxford University Press.

Martin, J. R. and Rothery, J. (1980) *Writing Project Report No. 1*. Sydney: University of Sidney, Department of Linguistics.

Martin, J. R. and Rothery, J. (1981) *Writing Project Report No. 2*. Sydney: University of Sidney, Department of Linguistics.

Martin, J. R. and Rothery, J. (1986) *Writing Project Report No. 4*. Sydney: University of Sidney, Department of Linguistics.

National Literacy Trust (2009) *Young People's Writing: Attitudes, Behaviour and the Role of Technology*. National Literacy Trust. Available online at: http://www.nationalliteracytrust.org.uk/research/Writing_survey_2009.pdf (accessed 16 January 2010).

Organisation for Economic Cooperation and Development (OECD) (2003) *Learners for Life: Student Approaches to Learning*. Paris: OECD Publications.

Palmer, S. (2001) *How to Teach Writing Across the Curriculum at Key Stage Two*. London: David Fulton.

Scott, P. (2001) 'Blogs in Education'. Available online at: http://www.det.wa.edu.au/education/cmis/eval/curriculum/ict/weblogs/ (accessed 15 August 2010).

Willett, R. (2009) 'Young people's video productions as new sites of learning', in V. Carrington and M. Robinson (eds), *Digital Literacies: Social Learning and Classroom Practice*. London: Sage.

Wray, D. (2006) *Teaching Literacy Across the Primary Curriculum*. Exeter: Learning Matters.

Wray, D. and Lewis, M. (1997) *Extending Literacy: Children Reading and Writing Non-Fiction*. London: Routledge.

Wray, D. and Lewis, M. (2004) 'Teaching factual writing: purpose and structure', in D. Wray (eds.), *Literacy: Major Themes in Education*. London: RoutledgeFalmer.

8

Lights, camera, action … take 9!

Tracy Parvin

Chapter Overview

A great deal has been written about the rapid advances which are being made in digital and Internet technologies and how these might impact not only on our modes of communication, but also on our perceptions of what literacy learning and teaching might now entail and the textual landscape that we inhabit both at home and in school. This chapter is based on an extended cross-curricular project which focused on non-fiction texts, culminating in the production of a digital video. Although the project took place in a Year 5 class, it must be stressed that the approach might be replicated in any year group. I shall begin by discussing the multi-modal aspects of communication which have become an element of today's society. I will also look at how, by introducing aspects of popular culture into the literacy curriculum, important home–school links might be forged and children's interests acknowledged. Consideration is also made as to how children's development of inference and deduction might be enhanced through the use of film. Throughout the course of the project three distinct themes, which are relevant to any similar project, emerged: group work, interaction and inclusion; immersion in texts; and knowledge of the audience and purpose. These will also be discussed.

The changing textual landscape

The latter end of the twentieth century saw a rapid increase in the everyday use of Internet and digital technologies. No longer are we limited to print-based texts as forms of communication; our literacy world has become multi-modal. Streets are filled with images, billboard advertisements, clothing logos, graffiti messages and posters, a visual attack on the senses. Meanwhile, music, whether it is advertising jingles or the latest R&B throb permeating through iPods or from passing cars, penetrates the ears. Text messages from mobile phones can be sent with appropriate images (emoticons) which ensure that the writer's, possibly brief, textual communication can nevertheless be fully interpreted by the reader (consider how the meaning of the words 'thank u so much' might be changed with the insertion of either a ☺ or ☹). The latest games for consoles can be trialled in numerous electrical retail outlets and magazine racks abound with literature aimed at users of gaming and computer technology; there are even Internet sites dedicated to any number of games, enabling the user to 'cheat' his way through the easy to the more challenging levels.

Inevitably, these items and their by-products make their way into the homes and lives of many of the children who inhabit our schools. As Carrington (2005: 13) suggests, the textual landscape which today's children now inhabit has 'implications for the skills and knowledge they bring with them to literacy instruction'. Image and sound have become an intrinsic constituent of the written word and serve to add further dimensions to printed text, an aspect of literacy of which today's children are keenly aware. Indeed, 'Children's familiarity with new forms of representation and communication means that they are thinking differently from those adults who were brought up in a more print-dominated world' (Bearne, 2003: 98). But to what extent can these media contribute to today's literacy curriculum and specifically to the teaching of non-fiction?

Research undertaken during the first few years of the millennium which focused on 'effective teaching' and 'effective teachers of literacy' (Wray et al., 2002) identified that the ability to articulate subject-specific pedagogic knowledge was essential to children's progress in reading and writing. However, while the research emphasised the importance of teachers possessing appropriate subject knowledge, the relevance of an understanding of popular culture, new media and digital literacies were completely bypassed, a deficit recognised by Bearne et al.:

> Such studies of effective teaching almost inevitably omit two important areas of teachers' professional capital: their knowledge of learners, and the cultures which surround the learning. (2003: 75)

It is necessary to look a little further along the library shelf in order to locate the researchers who do believe that a diverse array of textual modes can be used to enhance the literacy curriculum. Later in the chapter I hope to demonstrate just one way of achieving this.

Popular culture

It is not the intention here to discuss the many definitions of the concept of culture but rather to determine the nature of popular culture and, more importantly, children's popular culture. Developing an understanding of popular culture might enable you to consider how the literacy curriculum could be enhanced to reflect and build on the home literacy experiences of children. By its very definition, 'popular culture refers to aspects of culture shared by a large number of people' (Marsh and Millard, 2000: 17). It is generally not considered to be an elite form of culture; it is not opera, classical music or classic literary texts; rather it is popular music, magazines, computers, sport, television and film. Marsh and Millard (2000: 17) identify the overlap between adult popular culture and that of children, the difference being that 'children's popular culture also incorporates such diverse artefacts as toys, games, comics, stickers, cards, clothing, hair accessories, jewellery, sports accessories, oral rhymes, jokes, word play and even food and drink.' Once a craze has caught on there seems to be a never-ending availability of items associated with it, as 'The production of a new cultural icon is usually carried out after extensive market research' (Marsh and Millard, 2000: 20). It may well be that this overt consumerism deters some teachers from including aspects of popular culture in their literacy curriculum; it could be viewed as morally wrong to be appearing to endorse these expensive 'collectibles' (Grainger et al., 2005). Also, because cultural icons are constantly shifting, it is difficult for teachers to keep up with the latest crazes. It might be perceived that it is safer and easier to continue to teach along more traditional lines, ensuring optimum coverage of the curriculum while simultaneously protecting children from the ravages of consumerism.

However, it cannot be denied that children are enthused by popular cultural texts. In a survey undertaken in my Year 5 class, I wanted to determine what activities the children enjoyed at home in order to develop a clear picture of their literacy experiences. This can be a useful activity as it helps us to gain a greater understanding of what motivates the children to learn and the texts that they use at home in order to draw on their cultural and media interests within the literacy curriculum. As Haas Dyson suggests:

> We may begin by using children's experiences with media resources as bridges to a more traditional literacy curriculum. (Haas Dyson, 2004: x, cited in Evans, 2004)

The results of the survey showed that all pupils enjoyed not only playing a variety of games on consoles, listening to CDs and watching DVDs, videos and television programmes, but that they also read material associated with some of these leisure activities. A number of boys who mentioned that they enjoyed watching *Top Gear* also enjoyed reading Jeremy Clarkson books and *Top Car* magazines. Similarly a large number of both boys and girls enjoyed reading the Harry Potter books as well as watching the films and playing the console games. *Shrek* film and reading material featured largely in every response. Watching sport and reading sporting magazines was also a popular pastime. When asked specifically about home reading and writing activities, the list was almost endless: gaming tips, instructions on how to use MP3 players, instructions on how to download songs, TV magazines and schedules, comics, e-mails, texts, tags on clothes, CD cases, newspapers, school letters, cars on eBay, game cheats from the Internet, subtitles, pony magazines, menus, doodling, cards, song lyrics and books.

These are the children of the technological age; without realising it, they are using the tools available to them to help them to develop their skills and competencies in reading and writing, but with a purpose. These children are a far cry from the 'mindless zombies' which have been portrayed by some researchers (Healy, 1998) and in the tabloid media: they are interacting with today's technologies and they are using them to help them to be better informed. It would be a shame to confine these technologies to the home when they are having such a profound effect on the children's ability to learn. How then can popular culture texts be incorporated into the literacy curriculum and enhance children's learning? These were some of the questions that concerned me as I planned my own project for my class. Kellner (2003) suggests that if education is to be relevant to today's children, then educators should look at how media technologies could be integrated into the literacy curriculum. Our role as teachers of today's technological children is to be open to the technology available and identify its potential in the classroom.

Working with film

There are a range of researchers and theorists who advocate the importance of developing the higher-order reading skills of inference and deduction through film (BFI, 2003; Marsh, 2005; Larson and Marsh, 2005; Bearne and Wolstencroft, 2007; Stafford, 2011). Encouraging children to question the purposes of gestures, facial expressions, tone of voice and so on, and how these might be enhanced by camera shots and angles, lighting and non-diegetic sound, enables children to develop an understanding of directorial intent. These skills are transferrable to the written text and allow children to explore authorial intentions through choice of language. Incorporating film-making projects in the literacy curriculum, where children are creating their own visual texts, becomes a very powerful means of communication where the children become both author and director. Although film-making projects can aid children's development of narrative structure, they can also be used to enhance the non-fiction aspects of the literacy curriculum.

The project on which this chapter is based focused on a cross-curricular approach incorporating history, geography, ICT and, of course, literacy; the children were undertaking a historical research of their local area. Taking four buildings – an old Tudor-built house, a manor house, the church and the old Victorian school – plus the events surrounding the last battle on English soil, the children were able to construct a series of informative scripts derived from their researching of old documents and actual visits. The class was organised into five groups, each group taking responsibility for the research, compilation and presentation of information and filming of each diverse aspect of the project. The intention was then to disseminate this information, via a film, to an invited audience which included the rest of the school and parents and residents of the village; this decision proved to be an important aspect of the project. The members of each group determined the roles that were required and through discussion allocated themselves team-leading responsibility for a role for which they felt they had the appropriate skills and talents. The children decided that each group would need a researcher, script writer, presenters, director, cameraman and editor.

Research materials were obtained from a number of sources: local history pamphlets, Internet sites, old school log books, facsimiles of original documents from the Archive Library and interviews with the owners of the buildings. From this wide range of information, the script writers had to decide what it was the audience would like to know in order to create an illuminating and stimulating 'programme'. The cameramen and directors were given opportunities to visit the buildings beforehand to identify the best locations for filming; it was at this point that we realised that we would need a tripod and good weather! The class was also taught how to edit film by accessing the website http://www.channel4.com/learning/breakingthenews/index.html which has an online film and sound editing facility.

Throughout the whole process the class were completely engaged and focused; their intention of disseminating interesting historical information regarding their local area being fully realised in the production of a 'television programme'.

Having briefly talked you through one way of conducting a project like this, I will now discuss some of the issues that emerged and the particular aspects which are important considerations when working with children and film. One of the most important areas for consideration takes place during the initial planning stages.

Pre-planning preparation

- Determine what might motivate children; find out what their home literacy practices might be. This could be undertaken as a written survey, or simply through class discussion.

- Before planning for a multimedia project, consider the final outcome and how it will be presented. Will it, for instance, be a newspaper or magazine incorporating photographic images? A radio or television programme? An animated film? This is important as the final outcome will determine the equipment that you will be using.

- How will the children be organised? Will they be in pairs or groups or playing an individual role within a whole-class construction? Again, this is important as some pre-work might need to be undertaken to ensure that effective cooperative, collaborative and inclusive group work can take place.

Group work, interaction and inclusion

Grouping children for a project like this requires some careful consideration. In some schools it is the norm to group children according to attainment levels and ability for numeracy, literacy and guided reading, for instance. This form of grouping enables the teacher to provide appropriately targeted differentiated activities and scaffolded support. It could be argued, however, that a media project is best undertaken in mixed groups, enabling all children to enjoy the same sense of purpose, of working towards the same group outcome – for all children to feel as if they are making a purposeful contribution, playing to their own particular strengths and all being included. Children for whom English is an additional language (EAL) need to be grouped carefully according to their level and confidence with English. If possible, having more than one EAL pupil in a group (if they speak the same first language) can be helpful, as they can discuss ideas and support each other in their own language. Alternatively, ensuring that EAL pupils are in groups where the other children will provide useful role models and support can be a useful strategy.

Lachs (2000) considers the differences between cooperative and collaborative grouping for multimedia projects. She suggests that in cooperative groups the children work together towards a final outcome but are assigned different roles which do not overlap. Each person is responsible for their area of the project and work individually on this. This is the type of group construct which might be found in aspects of industry, such as the design or film-making industries. Collaborative grouping differs in as much as the group actually work together on *all* aspects of the project. The nature of the project might dictate the grouping approach that you use. The project upon which this chapter is based utilised a combination of cooperative and collaborative grouping, in as much as each child determined their role, for example researcher, writer, director, cameraman, presenter and editor. Instead of working independently from the rest of their group, however, they took the lead for the various aspects of the process while the other group members provided collegiate support. This enabled productive discussions to take place and for the whole group to become immersed in problem-solving activities throughout:

> ... they will all be involved in steering the course of the project and in doing a mixture of activities rather than confined to one. In collaboration each student will come up against others' views. They will need to be able to argue their own point of view, explain their own understanding and work out how these different points of view can work together. This will involve compromise and flexibility as well as combining ideas. (Lachs, 2000: 27)

I would argue that a project which is based on the necessity for successful collaborative work, such as a media project, encourages the children to engage in a wide range of problem-solving activities. This problem-solving approach also promotes the need for many group discussions and exploratory talk which permeate all stages of such a project. Barnes (2008) discusses the importance of exploratory talk and how it is a useful mechanism for developing understanding. His work focuses on children constructing meaning through talk – talk for thinking – but this does need appropriate planning and preparation. The potential for discussions to degenerate into disagreement is quite high and it might be wise to ensure that the appropriate classroom ethos which encourages supportive and profitable group discussions is firmly established. Mercer and Hodgkinson (2008) suggest that the teacher's influence in this is paramount, not only in modelling good social communications, but by actively developing approaches which ensure successful group work and exploratory talk. Too often teachers dominate the talking and engage children in question and answer activities where the questions that are asked are closed and require a predetermined answer. This form of speaking and listening repertoire does little to encourage a problem-solving exploration of possibilities (Barnes, 2008).

Corden (2000) suggests that exploratory talk between teachers and pupils and groups of pupils is a powerful means of learning. Being given opportunities to articulate ideas and thoughts and to develop these in a risk-free environment could enhance the understanding of sometimes difficult concepts; such discourse can enhance thinking and learning. This form of approach need not be confined to older year groups. Research undertaken by Tough (1977, cited in Corden, 2000) indicated that exploratory learning through verbal interactions can also be encouraged with very young children. However, developing the appropriate classroom ethos which encourages the children to participate in constructive discussion does require some thought and preparation. You might therefore want to consider the following:

- The type of questions that children are asked. Do your questions promote thinking? Questioning can be used in any subject. Even seemingly simple situations such as a shared reading experience could be an opportunity to promote a short discussion. Encourage children to explore particular aspects of an advertisement, for instance. Discuss what is being sold, the target audience and how this message is conveyed.

- Further develop a collegiate approach to speaking and listening activities. Generate a discussion which results in the children identifying and articulating their own and others' interests, talents and skills that they could bring to a diverse range of projects.

- Consider paving the way by developing shorter collaborative projects linked to aspects of the curriculum. Perhaps the children could engage in developing a group poster promoting a healthy lifestyle.

- Think about how you might want the groups constructed. Are you, as the teacher, going to group the children? This might be a useful approach for Early Years settings. Or will the children determine their own group construct? This could be established through class discussion. At this point, it is important that the children have an understanding of the task and the required skills; this will enable them to identify how they might be able to contribute to the project.

Immersion and interacting with the texts

As discussed in Chapter 1 of this book, it is essential to immerse children in texts. Such textual immersion enables children to assimilate the language to which they will have been exposed while simultaneously developing their own writing voices (Grainger et al., 2005); this is true of both fiction and non-fiction texts. Studying a range of non-fiction texts which are linked to other curriculum subjects, for instance history, geography or science, and then asking the children to present their findings in a different mode necessitates the exploration of a wider range of texts. For instance, if the children are going to engage in a filming activity, it will be useful to examine not only the original sources of the information but also the film or television genre that they will be using as the basis for their final presentation. My particular project focused on two diverse text types: a wide range of print-based authentic historical documents and also magazine-style television programmes which were chosen as the most appropriate genre of media broadcasting.

The historical documents which were studied included the witness statements taken during an inquest held in 1838 detailing the incidents leading up to a civil siege in the village, a military standoff and ultimately the death of a number of the rioters. The children also studied the Victorian school logs of their own school, which gave the day-to-day account of life in the school, the teachers, the children and descriptions of the lessons and also of unusual events, such as the chimney being struck by lightning. These logs enabled the children to make direct links and comparisons with their lives and the lives of the Victorian children who had once inhabited their school. The inquest report, on the other hand, fed their fertile imaginations – what really made the villagers riot? This was an area which the children keenly and critically explored. Studying the diverse perspectives and viewpoints that were given through the numerous words that had been spoken and recorded in May 1838 enabled the children to discuss their own opinions regarding the historical events. Having access to these documents gave the children a true sense of purpose; usually these artefacts were not on public display. The class, therefore, were going to be compiling their versions of local history to disseminate to a real audience, giving the project a sense of authenticity and relevance (Austin, 2005; Barnes, 2008).

The final outcome of a media project – how the children will present their findings – will also determine the range of multimodal texts that will be explored. For instance, if newspapers, comic strips or adverts are the media of choice, it is generally acknowledged that it is necessary to explore and analyse at a critical level how these forms of media inform, entertain or affect the audience and the modes of literacy which are incorporated to aid in the dissemination of information. The same could be suggested of the use of the moving image. The BFI publication 'Look Again!' (BFI, 2003) provides a very strong argument for viewing children's study and production of the moving image as an embedded literacy practice, rather than one which is dislocated, decontextualised or simply reduced to the watching of a film at the end of term (a well used practice in my own primary schooling).

As the final outcome for my project was to be the production of a 'television programme', it was necessary for the children to critically examine a range of programmes in order to determine and incorporate similar approaches and techniques in their own filming work. The programmes upon which we based our work were 'Coast' and 'The Holiday Programme'. In class we studied and analysed; the camera shots, the importance of location, how the presenters walked while simultaneously talking directly to their audience, when and why voice-overs were used and how the choice of language helped to maintain the audience's interest. Obviously, if you were to decide upon a different genre of filming, it would be equally important for the children to become immersed in and analyse the modes and filming techniques that signify that genre.

Knowledge of audience and purpose

The final theme that I want to discuss is the importance that having an authentic purpose alongside an understanding and knowledge of the intended audience play in the development of children's writing. As Lachs (2000) observes, usually the teacher is the only audience for children's work and that role is intertwined with that of assessor. This does have implications as to how children perceive their work, possibly believing that their teacher 'can fill in the gaps as well as correcting their spelling, punctuation and grammar' (Lachs, 2000: 51). However, the knowledge that their work is going to be communicated to a wider audience does have an impact on how that work is constructed. The children involved in this project would orally rehearse their scripts, identifying incorrect grammatical constructions, ensuring that the structure of their information had a sense of flow and that their vocabulary choices were appropriate for both the children and adult members of their audience. Whatever the situation, ensuring a real audience, (knowledge of which from the outset is of paramount importance) will give the children a true sense of purpose, and the more real the task, the more focused the children become. McGrath et al. (1997) suggests that presenting to a wider audience should help to improve children's attitude and approach to their task, the quality of their work and also encourage the sense of ownership. I can only support these observations, as the children in my class most certainly rose to the challenge in developing a well written, well presented, entertaining and informative project for their intended audience.

A final thought

A welcome by-product of a multimedia project in the classroom is that of having fun; not only the children, but also the teacher! It is possible that, alongside the children, you also will learn new skills. You might even find that, through their own explorations with the technology, the children might discover approaches that you had not considered and that they could end up teaching you a trick or two. How exciting is that?

Something to read

For further ideas, which are grounded in relevant theory, on how to incorporate a range of multi-modal practices in your classroom do have a look at Bearne and Wolstencroft's book *Visual Approaches to Teaching Writing*.

Something to think about

It is important to provide children with opportunities to develop their collaborative and group working skills. In this chapter I have emphasised the need to develop good group working conditions. Consider a range of methods and approaches that might work for you and your class.

Something to try

Explore the possibility of incorporating film-making into a range of curriculum areas. You could, for instance, get the children to prepare an advert which promotes a product which they have made in DT.

References

Alvermann, D. E., Moon, S. J. and Hagood, M. C. (1999) *Popular Culture in the Classroom: Teaching and Researching Critical Media Literacy*. Newark, NJ: International Reading Association.

Austin, R. (2005) 'You have been personally selected ... navigating non-fiction, negotiating modes: a critical response to real life', in A. Lambirth (ed.), *Planning Creative Literacy Lessons*. London: David Fulton.

Barnes, D. (2008) 'Exploratory Talk for Learning', in N. Mercer and S. Hodgkinson *Exploring Talk in School*. London: Sage.

Bearne, E. (2003) 'Rethinking literacy: Communication, representation and text' *Reading, Literacy and Language*, 37 (3).

Bearne, E. and Wolstencroft, H. (2007) *Visual Approaches to Teaching Writing: Multimodal Literacy 5–11*. London: Paul Chapman Publishing.

Bearne, E., Dombey, H. and Grainger, T. (eds) (2003) *Classroom Interactions in Literacy*. Maidenhead: Open University Press.

BFI (2003) *Look Again*. London: BFI Publications.

Carrington, V. (2005) 'New textual landscapes, information and early literacy', in J. Marsh (ed.), *Popular Culture, New Media and Digital Literacy in Early Childhood*. Abingdon: RoutledgeFalmer.

Corden, R. (2000) *Literacy and Learning Through Talk: Strategies for the Primary Classroom*. Buckingham: Open University Press.

Evans, J. (ed.) (2004) *Literacy Moves On: Using Popular Culture, New Technologies and Critical Literacy in the Primary Classroom*. David Fulton Publishers.

Grainger, T., Goouch, K. and Lambirth, A. (2005) *Creativity and Writing: Developing Voice and Verve in the Classroom*. London: Routledge.

Hannon, P. (2000) 'The history and future of literacy', in T. Grainger (ed.), *The RoutledgeFalmer Reader in Language and Literacy*. London: RoutledgeFalmer.

Healy, J. (1998) *Failure to Connect: How Computers Affect Our Children's Minds – And What We Can Do About It*. New York: Simon & Schuster Paperbacks.

Kellner, D. (2003) *New Media and New Literacies: Reconstructing Education for the New Millennium*. Online at: http://www.gseis.ucla.edu/courses/ed253a/kellner/newmedia. html (accessed 2 January 2008).

Kress, G. (2003) *Literacy in the New Media Age*. London: Routledge.

Lachs, V. (2000) *Making Multimedia in the Classroom*. London: RoutledgeFalmer.

Lambirth, A. (ed.) (2005) *Planning Creative Literacy Lessons*. London: David Fulton.

Larson, J. and Marsh, J. (2005) *Making Literacy Real: Theories and Practices for Learning and Teaching*. London: Sage.

Marsh, J. and Millard, E. (2000) *Literacy and Popular Culture: Using Children's Culture in the Classroom*. London: Paul Chapman.

Marsh, J. (ed.) (2005) *Popular Culture, New Media and Digital Literacy in Early Childhood*. Abingdon: RoutledgeFalmer.

McGrath, D., Cumaranatunge, C., Ji, M., Chen, H., Broce, W. and Wright, K. (1997) 'Multimedia science projects: seven case studies', *Journal of Research on Computing in Education*, 30 (1): 17–36.

Mercer, N. and Hodgkinson, S. (2008) *Exploring Talk in School*. London: Sage.

Stafford, T. (2011) *Teaching Visual Literacy in the Primary Classroom*. London: Routledge.

Wray, D. Medwell, J. Poulson, L. and Fox, R. (2002) *Teaching Literacy Effectively in the Primary School*. Language and Literacy in Action Series. London: RoutledgeFalmer.

9

Enhancing children's language acquisition and development through non-fiction

Virginia Bower

Chapter Overview

This chapter will examine how the use of non-fiction in the classroom can enhance children's language acquisition and development (highlighting strategies to use with children for whom English is an additional language). As with all the other chapters in this book, I shall emphasise the importance of using high-quality texts which motivate and inspire children, and which enable them to make links with their existing knowledge of the world and their life outside of the school environment. Although there will be a general discussion regarding non-fiction texts, the chapter will focus in more depth on the use of instructional texts and non-chronological texts and examples of children's work will be used to illustrate particular issues. Explicit links will be made between non-fiction and fiction and ideas provided as to how these two genres can be used together to provide children with an exciting and creative learning environment. The challenges which non-fiction texts can present will be discussed and examples will be given of how we can support the diverse needs of our pupils, including some ideas for writing frames to scaffold their written work.

Introduction

Children soon learn that language is their main way of communicating and a very effective tool for obtaining what they desire! This is true for those learning their first language (L1) and also for those learning a second language (L2), and usually it is the Basic Interpersonal Communication Skills (BICS) which EAL pupils pick up first to enable them to communicate and socialise with their peers (Cummins, 2001). Language is much more than this though. Vygotsky believed that language is a tool for thinking and that language use is inextricably linked with social and cultural experiences. He argued: 'Thought development is determined by language, i.e. by the linguistic tools of thought, and by the sociocultural experience of the child' (Vygotsky, 1962: 51). Once children begin school, they are quickly aware that they need to engage with 'school' language in order to fit into this new world:

> At school children have to learn to focus on language as the chief source of meaning. (Geekie et al., 1999: 67)

Although it is important to take into account and acknowledge children's home experiences, the fact is they have to learn how to fit into 'new functional registers or genres of language' (Cummins, 2001) and this is important for their school lives and beyond. As human beings we need to be familiar with both 'vernacular' and 'specialist' languages depending on specific situations. 'School is, as it is presently constituted, ultimately all about learning specialist varieties of language, in particular academic varieties of language connected to content areas' (Gee, 2004: 19). Children who have already had exposure to these more academic styles can be at an advantage in the classroom (Rosen, 2002). As creative teachers, we need to ensure that support is given to *all* children to enable them to engage with the variety of language they will encounter, and to promote a realisation that language, both oral and written, can empower us. Empowerment comes through being able to recognise the tone, style and features of language and to have the confidence to challenge and critically evaluate what others say and write. This develops through familiarity with a wide variety of texts.

Much of the language that children will encounter, particularly outside of the classroom, will be non-fiction and this will become more evident as they move towards adulthood:

> The bulk of adult experience with texts involve interactions with genres other than narrative. (Wray and Lewis, 1997: 2)

During a school day, it is likely that children will encounter a range of *fictional* texts, whether in shared and guided reading or independent 'silent' reading time or when they are writing their own stories. It is less common to see children being given non-fiction 'reading books', as many scheme, levelled and 'banded' books are fiction. There are, however, some commercial schemes which are beginning to include some excellent examples of non-fiction texts – Nelson Thornes produce the 'PM Books' which include non-fiction texts with wonderful photographs and topics which interest children. I have used this particular scheme with children and had great success; the books proved popular with both boys and girls and the children were very keen to take them home to share with their families. Aside from scheme books, however, our classrooms need to reflect the wonderful variety of non-fiction texts which are available and we need to ensure that they include examples from the range of non-fiction sub-genres.

The Primary National Strategy framework for literacy (DfES, 2006) identifies six key non-fiction categories:

- non-chronological reports

- persuasive texts

- explanation texts

- recounts

- discussion texts

- instructions.

Many teachers use this list to ensure that children are exposed to a range of non-fiction and it is important to have examples of high-quality texts which exemplify the features of each text type. If, for example, the chosen genre was persuasive texts, the class could create a book corner which contained examples of persuasive texts – both within books and also collected from the world around them in the form of advertisements, brochures, posters, persuasive letters. However, although the above list of text types is a good starting point, it is vital to think beyond this in order to make non-fiction relevant and pertinent to the lives of the children in your class. Be creative with your thinking and your choice of text. Many non-fiction texts do not conform to a specific genre and they often contain elements of a few. For example, a leaflet relating to a theme park will undoubtedly contain persuasive language, but it is also likely to contain many of the features of a non-chronological report or an explanation text, and will probably have some instructions relating to directions or payment. Do not let this deter you! This kind of text is going to be very familiar to children and they will implicitly know the typical linguistic features. Our job is to make the implicit explicit through discussion and critique of the text type. By drawing attention to specific linguistic features, we are empowering children in two key ways. Firstly, they begin to recognise when language has been used effectively and how this impacts upon the reader. Secondly, they begin to reflect this in their own writing as they are empowered by their knowledge about language and what it can do for them. The next section looks at some strategies for promoting this language awareness and provides some examples of a child's work to illustrate the power of non-fiction.

Strategies for promoting effective use of language in both L1 and L2 through non-fiction

Children will come into school with widely different experiences of language. Some will not have English as their first language; others will be members of very large families where their own voices are seldom heard; some will come from families where sitting down to a family meal is a daily occurrence and the place where talk is encouraged and whereby the child is exposed to an enhanced lexicon. In school, we need to provide an exciting environment, rich in a variety of languages and contexts to build upon children's myriad home experiences and to enable them to effectively communicate both orally and in the written form. Here are two approaches you might take when using non-fiction – one which makes use of unfamiliar material to inspire and excite children, and one which makes the most of children's existing knowledge to motivate them.

If the subject matter and the genre are unfamiliar, the teacher can introduce new language through the use of high-quality non-fiction texts, using these texts to immerse the children within the structure, form, register and linguistic features of the genre. An example of this could be non-chronological reports and the children might be encouraged to explore texts about animals from around the world that they have not encountered before. Inevitably, new vocabulary will emerge and while children are exploring a range of non-chronological reports and learning about these unfamiliar creatures, they will be absorbing the features of this particular genre. In this way, when the features are then addressed more explicitly, the children have both the vocabulary and the 'feel' of this text type. For children who have English as an additional language, specific vocabulary can be taught in advance so that they are more likely to be able to engage with the texts within the literacy lesson.

The other way to utilise non-fiction to promote language development is through subject matter which is already known to the children. An example of this – again with non-chronological texts – might be to set the class research projects where they have time to select a subject of their own choice, access a range of texts – books, websites, magazines, newspapers, encyclopaedias, etc. – collect information and then create their own non-chronological reports using the medium they prefer. This builds on children's existing knowledge, gives them choice and thereby relevance and enables them to make links with their own experiences both in and outside of school. In their book *City Literacies*, Eve Gregory and Ann Williams discuss how important it is to encourage children to 'syncretise or blend home, community and school language and cultural practices' (Gregory and Williams, 2000: xvii) and research within this type of project would promote this. In most cases, during their research and enquiry, children will encounter language they have not heard or used before and practitioners need to explicitly encourage them to explore this new vocabulary and use it in their own work. Pupils with EAL may find this type of task quite difficult as 'The lexicon used in English conversational interactions is dramatically different from than that used in more literate and academic contexts' (Cummins, 2001: 79). Because of this, EAL pupils need to read a great deal of written text (academic language) and to talk to peers and teachers about their reading, promoting higher-order thinking skills, thereby engaging in academic language and improving comprehension of what has been read. Often EAL pupils will have a good grasp of 'social' language but might struggle with vocabulary which is specific to a particular subject. Teacher language needs to be adjusted accordingly, as does the approach to teaching – using drama, visual prompts, tangible objects, etc. 'to make abstract concepts comprehensible' (Cummins, 2001: 83). Non-fiction texts – particularly non-chronological reports – can be beneficial here because they can be chosen for their relevance to and the needs of specific pupils. They very often contain pictures, photographs and visual cues which can aid understanding and, because they are factual, it is often easier to make the abstract concrete through the use of common knowledge. Other strategies can also be employed to support EAL pupils. They can be encouraged to create reports in their own language, perhaps choosing a topic which is pertinent to their own country, culture or tradition. Family members can be involved and if the opportunity arises, dual language texts and displays can be created, working together with the community. Dual language texts benefit all the children in the class as they raise awareness of similarities and differences between languages.

I would like to share an example which demonstrates how familiarity with and enthusiasm for a subject can be used to enable children to explore, recognise and use the typical linguistic features of a non-chronological report. The child I have chosen had a particular passion for horses and was very happy to be given the opportunity to do some research at home and write a non-chronological report on this subject. Here is a small section from her report:

> A horse is a large four legged mammal. If you have a horse you should feed it every day, three times a day; breakfast, lunch and dinner. Also mucking out and grooming should be done at least once a day.

> There is around 120 breeds of horse, these horses come in around 11 colours, which include: bay, brown, black, chestnut, white, dun, grey, roan, palomino, pinto (skewbald and piebald) and appaloosa. Some horses have facial and bodily markings.

In this piece of writing, the child has absorbed the style and tone of this text type and has adopted this, while demonstrating her own knowledge and understanding of the subject. The writing shows a grasp of some quite sophisticated punctuation and also an awareness of the possible lack of knowledge the reader might have – putting an explanation of 'pinto' in brackets. In this example, the 'pressure' is removed from the child in relation to subject matter and content – she is already confident and motivated to write about the subject. This gives her more 'mental space' for attending to the style, form and linguistic features of the genre. Frank Smith (1982) equates the compositional aspect of writing to the role of the author and the transcription aspect to that of the secretary. He gives particular responsibilities to the author and the secretary: the author collects ideas, selects words and considers grammar. The secretary focuses on the physical effort of writing, spelling, capitalisation, punctuation, paragraphs and legibility. By focusing on what is familiar, young writers have the opportunity to balance the attention they give to these two competing elements. Many of the boys in my class wrote reports based on football, and again, because they had the knowledge at their fingertips, they were able to concentrate on the form of the text type and produced some excellent pieces of writing.

The same child, at a later date, completed a timed assessment (along with the rest of the class) which involved writing a non-chronological report about beaches. The children had been studying geographical and geological features of beaches in other areas of the curriculum, but they did not have the opportunity to do personal research before writing. This is a small excerpt from her writing:

Beaches are found on the coasts of countries and are used in everyday life.

Some people depend on the sea for wealth, food and even their home. On the sea, fishermen in bad weather, risk life or death trying to feed their families and working for a living.

Beaches are great places to relax on, in the summer loads and loads of people come to beaches and swim, play in the sand, do donkey rides, funfairs or just sun bathe.

All over the world you can find caves; caves are sometimes man made, but most of all on coasts they are made by the sea. Caves are helpful to sea wildlife and can let birds lay eggs in and build nests. Caves are usually in the side of cliffs or at the bottom of them.

It can be seen in this extract, that, once again, the pupil has been able to adopt the style and tone of a report and used some of the key features – moving from the generic to the specific for example – and has used her newly acquired knowledge and vocabulary. These two examples demonstrate how, by giving children the freedom initially to write about a subject of their choice, they can then utilise what they have learnt in a new context. Bruner (1966) characterises intellectual growth as a developing independence which enables the learner to make use of knowledge that has been stored internally, and to apply that knowledge in new contexts, making effective use of language. The use of non-fiction is an exciting way to promote this intellectual growth.

Fiction and non-fiction – making links

In this section, I shall use three particular texts to demonstrate how fiction and non-fiction can successfully and creatively support each other and thereby provide children with an incredibly rich learning environment. The first text is *Beware of Boys* by Tony Blundell, a text which, at first glance, is merely about a boy who manages to 'get one over' an unsuspecting wolf, but which, on repeated reading, offers far, far more than this. There is humour, irony, word play, subversion and the triumph of brains over greed to name but a few features! However, my focus is on the non-fiction elements of the text – recipes – which would fall within the instructional non-fiction sub-genre. There are three recipes in the book – Boy Soup, Boy Pie and Boy Cake – and all three are set out in exactly the same way with a list of ingredients, a set of instructions entitled 'Method' and pictures to support. The recipes have all the linguistic features of typical instructional texts: clear descriptions of the ingredients including amounts and colourful use of alliterative language – 'One oodle of onions', 'One big blob of butter'; imperative verbs, for example 'place', 'add' and 'wash'; adverbs to reinforce the method – 'firmly', 'thoroughly' and 'carefully'; and numbers and temporal indicators to reinforce order and timing. The ingredients appear to be random, crazy objects (but all becomes clear at the end of the story) and children love to consider the vast quantities described – 'One binful of brown sugar' and 'One wheelbarrow of walnuts' for example. They can then go on to create their own list of ingredients for a particular recipe – this could be a recipe for a fairytale character – perhaps a friend for the Gingerbread Man in the form of a giant cookie, or a cake for Little Red Riding Hood to take when she visits her grandma. They might choose to set out their list in the same way as the author does in 'Beware of Boys' and create illustrations alongside in the same way. They could then move on to the 'Method' and they could explore in books and online to see the different ways that writers tend to set out their instructions – these might be in picture form without any words, or in bullet-pointed lists, numbered instructions, diagrams, descriptive paragraphs, etc. Give the children the opportunity to choose the format that best suits their recipe and ensure that they have the time to research and immerse themselves in the instructional genre. The children's recipes could be put together to make a class book and at a later date, perhaps when the class is focusing on narrative writing, the children might want to create a story wherein their recipes occur, in the same way as Tony Blundell.

The next text I would like to recommend is *Meerkat Mail* by Emily Gravett. This is a wonderful, high-quality text with incredible illustrations and enough elements to give you ideas for a whole unit of work! It has a common theme of someone – Sunny the Meerkat – who is dissatisfied with his life and his family and decides to find a better place to live, only to find that the grass is certainly not greener on the other side! Along the way, Sunny writes notes and postcards back to his family and these mini-texts within the main text are one of the non-fiction elements. The postcards have numerous features which are common to many non-fiction texts in our everyday lives. The initial note left by Sunny is written as an informal letter (although it has a very formal letter heading in the form of the meerkat motto – STAY SAFE STAY TOGETHER) which starts 'Dear Everyone' and ends 'Love from Sunny'. It has a 'P.S.' and also contains a crossed out list where Sunny has written a reminder note to himself of what to pack. Just with this one note there is much to discuss in the classroom and children could be encouraged to bring in notes that members of their families write at home – perhaps shopping lists, reminders, to do lists, notes on fridge doors – so that it is relevant to their own lives. The informal language and register of this type of text can be noted and the very personal nature of the content. Throughout the book, Sunny sends postcards back to his family and this provides a great link with children's own experiences of sending and receiving postcards. Again, they can be encouraged to bring in examples from home and the style and tone of the language can be investigated. If possible, after a school outing, children could be encouraged to write their own postcards, describing their experiences, or they could send an e-mail to a family member or a friend detailing the event. This is usually very successful, particularly if the recipients can be encouraged to write back and a regular correspondence set up. This provides the audience and purpose which is so essential for any form of writing. At the very end of *Meerkat Mail*, there are more examples of non-fiction mini-texts. There is a travel 'photocard', which could be compared and contrasted with passports; there are photographs with captions beneath; and there is a newspaper article with the headline 'SUNNY COMES HOME!' which not only has a report written in typical newspaper style, but also has a small advertisement which is a good example of persuasive language. This book really does have it all!!

The final text – *Jennifer Jones Won't Leave Me Alone* by Frieda Wishinsky and Neal Layton – is a truly multi-modal text with amazing potential. It manages to combine the three main genres – narrative, poetry and non-fiction – in one dazzling text with the most wonderful illustrations which include cartoon-like pictures and real-life photographs. One of the main characters leaves her friend to go on a world tour and she sends back postcards describing her adventures. There are also examples of metro bus and subway tickets, addressed envelopes and photographs of coins from around the world. This text could form the basis for work on non-chronological reports, with children choosing a country that they have visited or would like to visit and collecting information from different sources about their chosen place. They could bring in photographs, coins, post-cards, etc. from home and these could be incorporated within their reports to make their own multi-modal texts. If you have children from other countries or from different regions in your class, they could be encouraged to share their knowledge and experience and to teach the other children about their own language (their non-chronological reports could be dual language texts), the geographical features of their home place, traditions, etc. Because these texts will be multi-modal and not entirely reliant on the written word, they are a more accessible task for all members of your class.

Using non-fiction – the challenges

Using non-fiction in the classroom is an excellent means by which children can learn about the power of language and presents us with wonderful, exciting ways to promote a higher level of language use. It does, however, have its challenges:

- Non-fiction often contains subject-specific vocabulary which can be difficult for children to access, particularly if English is not their first language.

- Classrooms may not contain the diversity of texts that you need to teach non-fiction effectively – it is more common to find a wide range of fictional texts.

- It may not be immediately obvious how exciting activities can be linked with non-fiction, i.e. drama, role-play, use of film, etc.

- Often we encourage children to do their own research towards a non-fiction project. Unfortunately, this often results in pupils printing off vast quantities of text from Internet sites which they may not have read or understood.

- Sometimes we lack confidence in our own knowledge and understanding of the linguistic features of particular non-fiction text types and this can restrict our approach to the learning and teaching.

Here are some ideas to help with these challenges:

- *Word banks/lists*. As soon as you begin a new non-fiction topic, create a word bank which is highly visible within the classroom. This will be added to as the unit progresses (by you and the children). If you do this as you go along, it gives you the opportunity to find ways to make the vocabulary accessible (if possible, providing translations of key words for EAL pupils).

- *Working walls*. A working wall can be very useful to support children with new concepts and it allows them to be actively involved. This can either be an actual piece of wall space or a flip chart page which has the title of the genre under study, i.e. Instructional Texts. On to this you can place word lists, examples of children's work, items that the pupils have brought from home, i.e. recipes, game instructions, top tips for writing, examples of particular linguistic features, i.e. imperative verbs, etc. Because the children are involved in constantly adding to the wall, they feel an ownership which leads to more of a tendency to use this resource when they are tackling their own writing.

- *Writing frames*. These can be very useful to scaffold children's writing and can be differentiated to provide different levels of support. See Figure 9.1 for an example of a writing frame which links with the text *Beware of Boys* which was discussed in an earlier section.

- *Supporting materials*. Provide plenty of tangible objects which bring the language 'to life', i.e. recipe books/cards, leaflets, household products which have examples of relevant language, electronic games with instructions, encyclopaedias, books of facts, etc.

RECIPE TITLE

INGREDIENTS

METHOD

First...

Then..

Next..

After that...

USEFUL VOCABULARY

Place
Add
Stir
Measure
Weigh
Bake
Temperature
Oven
Kilogram

Figure 9.1   Example of a writing frame

- *Drama, role-play and film.* It may not be as obvious to use these practices for non-fiction as it is for fiction but be creative in your thinking! If the children are learning about persuasive texts, it would be very useful for them to engage in process drama, thinking about the language they need to use to persuade someone to do something. Equally, film can be very useful to illustrate particular text types. Children could watch a cookery programme, looking out for instructional language; they might watch an episode from *Blue Peter* to see how someone explains a process. They might then go on to make their own films based on a particular non-fiction text type.

- *Researching from the Internet.* Children need to have specific instruction about how to collect information from websites. You need to be sure that they are reading the text, evaluating its usefulness and extracting only the parts that they need (preferably putting this into their own words). The method I used was to ensure that children always had a Word document open as well as a website. Each time they found something useful, they put a few notes onto the Word document (not necessarily full sentences), which they could then use at a later date for their own writing.

- *Building our own confidence.* Make sure that you are confident and comfortable with the linguistic features of particular text types. *Grammar for Writing* (DfEE, 2000) is a useful document which defines the non-fiction genres and provides ideas for activities.

Conclusion

I do not believe it is possible to overstate the importance of supporting children with their development of language. Much of this can be done through narrative – enjoying and sharing stories which provide not only new words but new worlds to explore and lose yourself in. However, non-fiction has an equally important role and, for many children, will provide the relevance and authenticity they need to engage and interest them. Non-fiction texts are an integral part of our everyday lives and yet children may be unaware of their prominence and significance. By raising this awareness, young learners become more attuned to their environment, recognising when they are being persuaded or coerced, understanding when texts are biased or unreliable, and realising the true potential and power of language and what it can do for them. As Margaret Meek says:

> The most important single lesson that children learn from texts is the nature and variety of written discourse, the different ways that language lets a writer tell, and the many and different ways a reader reads. (Meek, 1988: 21)

A valuable lesson to learn.

Something to read

Extending Literacy: Children Reading and Writing Non-Fiction by David Wray and Maureen Lewis is an excellent text based on research undertaken as part of the Exeter Extending Literacy (EXEL) Project.

Something to think about

How many times a day do you engage with non-fiction text types? Think about the effect these texts have on your life and encourage the children in your class to do the same.

Something to try

Hold a 'Non-fiction Day' in your school, encouraging pupils to bring in texts from home, making food from instructional recipes, sharing facts from favourite sources, celebrating the language and information to be gained from this genre.

References

Bruner, J. (1966) *Towards a Theory of Instruction.* Cambridge, MA: Belknap Press.

Cummins, J. (2001) *Language, Power and Pedagogy.* Clevedon: Multilingual Matters.

DfEE (2000) *Grammar for Writing.* London. HMSO.

DfES (2006) *Primary National Strategy: Primary Framework for Literacy and Mathematics.* Nottingham: DfES Publications.

Gee, J. P. (2004) *Situated Language and Learning.* New York and London: Routledge.

Geekie, P., Cambourne, B. and Fitzsimmons, P. (1999) *Understanding Literacy Development.* London: Trentham.

Gregory, E. and Williams, A. (2000) *City Literacies: Learning to Read Across Generations and Cultures.* London and New York: Routledge.

Meek, M. (1988) *How Texts Teach What Readers Learn.* Exeter: Thimble Press.

Rosen, M. (2002) *Did I Hear You Write?* Nottingham: Five Leaves.

Smith, F. (1982) *Writing and the Writer.* London: Heinemann Educational.

Vygotsky, L. S. (1962) *Thought and Language.* Cambridge, MA: MIT Press.

Wray, D. and Lewis, M. (1997) *Extending Literacy: Children Reading and Writing Non-Fiction.* London and New York: Routledge.

Children's literature

Beware of Boys by Tony Blundell

Meerkat Mail by Emily Gravett

Jennifer Jones Won't Leave Me Alone by Frieda Wishinsky and Neal Layton

Index

A
adult popular culture, overlap between children's and 78
'apprentices in workshop' model 46
assessment 9
Audacity 70
audience, knowledge of 83–4
authentic purpose, importance 83–4
authors
    adoption of the styles of 7
    see also single author studies
autobiographical writing *see* writing from experience

B
Basic Interpersonal Communication Skills (BICS) 86
Beware of Boys 90–1, 93
blogging 70–1
bodily activity, oral communication through 58
boys, and violent playground games 37
Brownjohn, Sandy 46, 48
Bruner, J. 57, 90

C
challenging subjects, considering 27, 28
chanting, singing and 59, 61–2
children
    as 'conscious artists' 46
    as storytellers 17–18
children with English as an additional language (EAL) *see* EAL (English as an additional language) learners
children as writers 26–30
    helping development of 29
children's popular culture
    differences between adult and 78
    and playground games 37, 41
    use in the classroom 37–8, 78–9
children's writing
    enhancing 3–10
    impact of powerful literature 5–7
    and knowledge of audience and purpose 83–4
choosing rhymes 40
Cinderella
    comparing different versions 15–16
        using literature Venn diagrams 16
    and cross-curricular links 20
City Literacies 89
clapping rhymes 36–7, 39
    differentiating between skipping and 42
classroom drama *see* process drama

collaborative grouping for multimedia projects, differences between cooperative and 81
collaborative writing 47
communication
    and film-making projects 79
    language and 86
    multi-modal aspects 77–8
    see also oral communication
'concept builders' xiii
conscience tunnels 61
'conscious artists', children as 46
consumerism and popular culture 78
contextualisation
    importance 8–9
    and non-fiction 67, 69, 72
    and the process approach to writing 25
cooperative grouping for multimedia projects, differences between collaborative and 81
creation myths 13
creative teaching xiii
'Creativity and Writing' 27
Creativity and Writing: Developing Voice and Verve in the Classroom 27
cross-curricular activities
    Cinderella and 20
    non-fiction and 72–3
        film-making project 80, 83
Crossley-Holland, Kevin 4, 5, 6, 7
cultural activities, internalization of 57–8
cultures
    exploring Cinderella stories from different 15–16
        using literature Venn diagrams 16
    exploring diversity within xiv, 16–17
    understanding between 14
    see also popular culture
'curriculum deliverers' xiii

D
decision alley and discursive writing 71
deduction, development through film-making 79
Desperate Measures 27
digital technologies
    everyday use 77–8, 79
    see also ICT; Internet
discursive writing, decision alley and 71
drama
    and non-fiction 71–2, 94
    traditional tales as a stimulus 18–19
    see also process drama
dual language texts 89

E

EAL (English as an additional language)
  learners
    and groupings for multimedia
      projects 81
    learning a second language 86
    and non-fiction xv, 88, 89
    and playground games 41
    and poetry writing 50
    and storytelling 16–17
Early Years Foundation Stage 71
effective teaching, studies of 78
empowerment
    language and 87, 88
    through engagement with texts 3
    through poetry writing 47
experience, writing from *see* writing from
    experience
experienced readers 4
exploratory talk 81–2
eye-witness report writing within a
    historical context 72–3

F

fables 13
fairy stories 14
    difference between folk tales and 14
fiction, making links with non-fiction 90–2
film-making
    non-fiction 79–80, 94
    see also non-fiction film-making project
folk tales 13–14
    difference between fairy stories and 14
    'trickster' characters 14
    see also Cinderella
freeze frames 61
    instructional writing and 71
functional approach to language 23

G

gender divide
    and non-fiction reading 74
    in playground games 36
gender roles, in traditional tales 15
Genre Studies 30
genre-led literacy xiv, 23–5
    benefits 24
    choice of text types 25, 30
    countering over-use 29
    disadvantages 24–5
'good' writing, perceptions 8
grammar, teaching of 8
Grammar for Writing 68
Grimm, Jacob and Wilhelm 14
group work for multimedia projects
    81, 82
guided writing sessions 48

H

Halliday, Michael 23
historical context, eye-witness report
    writing within 72–3

home
    and experience of language 87, 88
    use of technologies 79
    writing at *see* out-of-school writing
home-school links
    and playground games 37, 39
    through reading 10
hot-seating 61
    and recount writing 71
Hughes, Ted 46

I

ICT
    and non-fiction 70–1
      blogging 70–1
      using podcasts 70
    pervasiveness of 70
    see also digital technologies; Internet
'imaginary games' 37
immersion in texts 4, 9, 82, 88
inclusion
    and multimedia projects 81–2
    through modelling poetry 50
Indian myths 13
inference, development through film-
    making 79
instructional writing, freeze frames and 71
intellectual growth 90
interaction in multimedia projects 81–2
interactive responses, and poetry
    writing 47
internalization of cultural activities 57–8
Internet
    everyday use 77–8, 79
    researching non-fiction from 92, 94
    see also blogging; podcasts
Into the Woods 20
Irish myths 13
issues, dealing with 27, 28

J

Jennifer Jones Won't Leave Me Alone 91–2
jumping games 36–7

K

kenning poems 48–9
knowledge
    and the cross-curricular approach to
      writing non-fiction 73
    through social interaction 57–8

L

language
    empowerment and 87, 88
    functional approach 23
    home experience 87, 88
    variety 87
language acquisition and development
    86–95
    and non-fiction 87, 88–90
      challenges 92
      making links with fiction 90–2

language acquisition and development *cont.*
    making use of unfamiliar material 88, 90
    techniques to support 92–4
    using existing knowledge 88–90
  play and 35–6
'language of power' 68
language of traditional tales 14
learning
  motivation and 72
  physical approaches 71
    and poetry 58
  play and 35
  through exploratory talk 82
  through performance poetry 57–8
  using playground games 42–3
legends 13
life experiences
  linking traditional tales with 20
  linking writing and *see* writing from
    experience
literature Venn diagrams, using 16
'Look Again!' 83

M
The Magic Box 50
'Me', use of teacher-in-role 60–1
Meerkat Mail 91
meetings, and poetry process drama
  (PPD) 60
memorising poetry 59
Mesopotamian myths 13
metaphor, play and 45, 46
modelling poetry 47–8, 49–51
Morpurgo, Michael 26–7
motivation, as the key to learning 72
movement, and songs and rhymes 36
Mufaro's Beautiful Daughters 15
multimedia projects
  groupwork, interaction and inclusion
    81–2
  immersion and interacting with texts
    82, 83
  and knowledge of audience and
    purpose 83–4
  pre-planning preparation 80
  presentation of findings 83
music 36
myths 13

N
National Curriculum, addressing
  objectives 40–1
National Literacy Strategy (NLS) xiii, 23
  and non-fiction 67
non-chronological reports, and promoting
  effective use of language 88–90
non-fiction 67–75
  and cross-curricular activities 72–3
  genres 68–9, 87–8
  and language acquisition and
    development *see* language acquisition
    and development, and non-fiction

non-fiction *cont.*
  motivating learners
    role of ICT *see* ICT, and non-fiction
    using drama 71–2, 94
    using experiences and interests 69–70
  selecting texts 73–4
non-fiction film-making 79–80, 94
non-fiction film-making project xv, 80
  grouping approach 81
  immersion and interacting with the
    texts 82–3
  and knowledge of audience and
    purpose 83–4
Norse myths 13

O
oral communication, through bodily
  activity 58
oral text 5
oral tradition of storytelling 12, 14, 15, 20
'oral writing' 46
out-of-school writing 27–8
  as the voice of the child 28

P
'passive experiences', impact on
  learning 71
performance drama 18
performance poetry xiv, 55–63
  categorising 58–62
    poetry process drama (PPD) 59, 60–1
    singing and chanting 59, 61–2
    slamming 56, 58–60
  and learning 57–8
  as response 56–8
The Persian Cinderella 15, 16
  and cross-curricular work 20
persuasive texts 88
physical approaches to learning 71
  and poetry 58
Pirrie, Jill 46, 52
play
  and language acquisition 35–6, 71
  and learning 35
  and metaphor 45, 46
playground games xiv, 35–43
  boys' 37
  case study 38–43
  effect of popular culture 37
  gender divide 36
  and promoting home-school links 37
  teaching 37
  types 36
playground rhymes 36–7, 61
  case study 39–43
    utilizing and transforming ideas 40–2
  differentiating between skipping and
    clapping 42
  learning through 42–3
  and poetry slamming 60
playgrounds, as unhappy spaces 38
'PM Books' 87

PNS xiii, 23
  non-fiction categories 87
podcasts, using 70
poetic forms xiv, 45–53
  as an inclusive approach 50
  kenning poems 48–9
  techniques to support use 47–8
  viewpoints relating to 45–7
poetic voice, developing 45, 47, 49
poetry
  exposing children to 56–7
  memorising 59
  modelling 47–8, 49–51
  multi-modal nature 56
  performing *see* performance poetry
  use of physical movement in
    composition 58
poetry process drama (PPD) 59, 60–1
poetry slams 56, 58–60
popular culture
  children's *see* children's popular culture
  definition 78
  differences between adult and
    children's 78
power of text 3–5
powerful literature
  defining 4
  finding and utilising 8, 9
  impact on children's writing 5–7
practice
  linking theory with xiii
  research and xiii
Primary National Strategy *see* PNS
PrimaryBlogger 71
problem-solving in multimedia projects
    81–2
process approach to writing 25–6
  benefits 26
  criticisms 26
process drama 18, 60
  use for non-fiction 94
  see also poetry process drama (PPD)
prosodic features, influence 6, 7
purpose, knowledge of 83–4

R
re-reading stories 7
readers, *experienced* 4
reading
  gap between writing and 8
  link with writing 4, 5
  linking lives outside school with 10
reading aloud 4–5
  see also storytelling
recount writing, hot-seating and 71
research, grounding theory and practice
    in xiii
rhymes 36, 57
  see also playground rhymes
role play, and non-fiction 71–2, 94
role on the wall 61
Rosen, Michael 36, 46, 61–2

The Rough-Face Girl 15–16
  and cross-curricular work 20
  ideas for drama using 19

S
scaffolding, and the use of poetic forms 51
scheme books 87
'school' language 86–7
school, promoting links between home
    and *see* home-school links
'scripted' stories 7
second language, strategies for promoting
    language use 88, 89
shared writing 47
singing and chanting 59, 61–2
single author studies xiv, 3–10
  choosing texts and authors 10
  and links to life experiences 6–7
  promoting appreciation of chosen
    authors 4
  and teaching technical aspects of
    writing 8–9
skipping rhymes 36–7, 39–40
  differentiating between clapping rhymes
    and 42
  to encourage poetry slamming 60
slam poetry 56, 58–60
social interaction, knowledge through 57–8
songs 36
  see also rhymes
'specialist' language 87
stereotyping in traditional tales 15
stories
  creating own versions of 7
  re-reading 7
story drama *see* process drama
story hands 18
story mountains 18
story plates 18
storytellers, teachers and children as 17–18
storytelling 16–17
  oral tradition 12, 14, 15, 20
  and supporting EAL (English as an
    additional language) learners 16–17
  see also reading aloud
structure of traditional tales 14
Summers, Laura 27

T
'task managers' xiii
teacher-in-role, in poetry process drama
    (PPD) 60–1
teachers, as storytellers 17
technical aspects of writing, teaching 8–9
television programmes, use in language
    and literacy planning 37–8
text, power of 3–5
text types, teaching using *see* genre-led
    literacy
'texts that teach' 5
textual immersion 4, 9, 82, 88
textual landscape, changing 77–8

themes in traditional tales 14, 15
theory
    linking practice with xiii
    research and xiii
thought development and language 86
thought-tracking 61
The Three Rival Brothers 15
    ideas for drama using 19
traditional tales xiv, 12–21
    exploring cultural diversity through xiv,
        14, 16–17
    oral nature 12, 14, 15, 20
    stereotypical representation of gender
        roles 15
    as a stimulus for drama 18–19
    themes, structure and language 14–15
    types 12–14
        blurring of boundaries between 12–13
Twelve Months 16

V
'vernacular' language 87
voice
    developing 3, 26, 29
    importance 23
    out-of-school writing as 28
    through playground games 41
    see also poetic voice; reading aloud
Vygotsky, L. S. 57, 86

W
'We're Writers' 27
Wilson, Jacqueline 27
word banks/lists 92
working walls 92–3
writers, children as *see* children as writers
writing 9
    approaches 23–6
        using a mixture 30
    by children *see* children's writing
    gap between reading and 8
    link with reading 4, 5
    linking life experiences and 6–7
    modelling 47–8
    out-of-school *see* out-of-school writing
    perceptions of 'good' 8
    teaching technical aspects 8–9
    see also collaborative writing; discursive
        writing; instructional writing; 'oral
        writing'; recount writing; shared
        writing
writing frames 24, 93
writing from experience 6–7, 23–31,
    26–7
    non-fiction writing 69–70, 89–90
    poetry writing 47, 52
writing journals 29
writing notebooks 27
writing workshops 29

YOUNG CHILDREN READING

At home and at school

Rachael Levy *University of Sheffield*

Developing and supporting literacy is an absolute priority for all early years settings and primary schools, and something of a national concern. By presenting extensive research evidence, Rachael Levy shows how some of our tried and tested approaches to teaching reading may be counter-productive, and are causing some young children to lose confidence in their abilities as readers. Through challenging accepted definitions and perspectives on reading, this book encourages the reader to reflect critically on the current reading curriculum, and to consider ways in which their own practice can be developed to match the changing literacy landscape of the 21st century.

Placing the emphasis on the voices of the children themselves, the author looks at:

- what it feels like to be a reader in the digital age
- children's perceptions of reading
- home and school reading
- reading in multidimensional forms
- the future teaching of reading.

Essential reading for all trainee and practising teachers, this critical examination of a vital topic will support all those who are interested in the way we can help future generations to become literate. This book will encourage researchers and practitioners alike to redefine their own views of literacy, and situate 'reading literacy' within the digital world in which young children now live.

July 2011 • 168 pages
Cloth (978-0-85702-990-4) • £65.00
Paper (978-0-85702-991-1) • £20.99

ALSO FROM SAGE